GREAT Sales Coaching Unleashing Your Retail Team's Potential

Turn Managers into Coaches.

Turn Sales Associates into Sales Champions.

By Matthew Hudson, PhD

Order other books by Matthew on Amazon.com

Culturrific!
Creating an experiential culture in your organization.
$19.95

The Retail Sales Bible
The G.R.E.A.T. Selling System for Retail. Written for retail sales professionals.
$19.95

Advisor Selling
The art and science of becoming a trusted sales advisor. Written for B2B sales reps.
$19.95

Signs Sell
Harnessing the Power of Your Interior Advertising
$25.95

Herd Mentality: Leadership Lessons from Rescue Horses
Proceeds Benefit the Layla Rose Ranch Horse Rescue
$20.00

GREAT Sales Coaching
Unleashing Your Retail Team's Potential

Copyright © 2025 Matthew Hudson
All rights reserved. No part of this publication may be reproduced, distributed or transmitted in any form or by any means, including photocopying, recording, or other electronic or mechanical methods, without the prior written permission of the publisher, except in the case of brief quotations embodied in critical review and certain other noncommercial uses permitted by copyright law. Rights to the signs used in this book for illustration purposes are the property of the company that created them.

Request for permission should be sent to:
matt@hudsonhead.com
Annetta, Texas 76008

Printed in the United States of America
ISBN 978-0-9719731-5-2
Library of Congress 2025921671

Contents

Preamble .... Page 6

Part 1 - The GREAT Sales Coaching Framework

Chapter 1: The Foundation of Sales Leadership .... Page 10
- Why coaching Matters More Than Management

Chapter 2: The GREAT Coaching Framework .... Page 18
- Your Five-Step System to Success

Chapter 3: Get Ready (Prepare) .... Page 28
- Setting the Stage for Learning Excellence

Chapter 4: Reveal Through Demonstration (Demonstrate) .... Page 38
- The Art of Showing the Way

Chapter 5: Engage Through Practice (Have Them Do It) .... Page 48
- Active Learning Through Practice

Chapter 6: Affirm and Encourage (Keep It Positive) .... Page 58
- The Psychology of Reinforcement

Chapter 7: Track Progress (Follow Up) .... Page 68
- Ensuring Long-Term Success and Growth

Part 2 - Achieving Success with GREAT Sales Coaching

Chapter 8: Overcoming Resistance......................................Page 79
- Dealing with Change and Fear

Chapter 9: Role-Play..Page 96
- Making Practice Perfect

Chapter 10: Building a Culture of Continuous Improvement..................Page 109
- Intrinsic Motivation

Chapter 11: Advanced Coaching Techniques...............................Page 125
- Adapting to Different Learning Styles

Chapter 12: Measuring Success...Page 138
- Metrics That Matter in Sales Coaching

Chapter 13: The Role of the GREAT Sales Coach..........................Page 151
- From Commanding to Developing

Postscript...Page 164

References..Page 168

About the Author..Page 170

Preamble

In the bustling world of retail, where competition is fierce and Customer expectations continue to rise, one truth remains constant: the difference between mediocre and exceptional performance lies not in the products on the shelves, but in the people behind the counter. While retailers scramble to match each other on merchandise selection, pricing, and store ambiance, the most successful ones have discovered a secret weapon that their competitors often overlook—their sales team's knowledge, skills, and motivation.

This book is about transforming ordinary sales associates into extraordinary sales professionals through the power of coaching. It's about moving beyond the traditional command-and-control management style that stifles creativity and initiative and embracing a coaching approach that unleashes the untapped potential within every team member.

The retail landscape has evolved dramatically over the past decade. Online shopping, price comparison apps, and changing consumer behaviors have fundamentally altered how people shop. In this new reality, the role of the sales associate has become more critical than ever. They are no longer just order-takers or cash register operators; they are consultants, problem-solvers, and brand ambassadors who can make or break the Customer experience.

Yet, despite this elevated importance, many retail organizations continue to treat their sales staff as replaceable parts rather than valuable assets worthy of investment and development. This approach is not only shortsighted but also counterproductive in today's competitive marketplace. The retailers who thrive are those who recognize that their greatest competitive advantage lies in developing their people.

The **GREAT** Sales Coaching system outlined in this book represents a fundamental shift in how we think about sales leadership. It's based on the understanding that coaching is not just about correcting mistakes or pushing for better numbers—it's about unleashing human potential, building confidence, and creating a culture where continuous improvement is not just encouraged but expected.

Throughout these pages, you'll discover that coaching is equal parts art and science. It requires technical knowledge of sales processes and techniques, but it also demands emotional intelligence, patience, and the ability to see potential where others might see problems. The best sales coaches are those who can balance high expectations with genuine support, who can be tough on performance standards while remaining compassionate toward the person behind the performance.

This book will take you on a journey from understanding the fundamental principles of effective sales coaching to mastering advanced techniques that can transform even the most reluctant team members into engaged motivated performers. You'll learn not just what to do, but why it works, drawing on insights from psychology, neuroscience, and decades of real-world experience in retail environments.

Whether you're a new manager taking on your first coaching role, an experienced leader looking to refine your approach, or a senior executive seeking to build a coaching culture throughout your organization, this book provides the roadmap you need to succeed. The principles and techniques you'll learn here are not theoretical concepts dreamed up in an ivory tower—they're battle-tested strategies that have been proven to work in the trenches of retail sales floors across the country.

To accomplish this task, the book is divided into two parts. Part I is the overview and explanation of the **GREAT** Sales Coaching framework. Part II is a deep dive into some of the key principles and tools used in the framework like roleplay.

As we embark on this journey together, remember that becoming a great sales coach is itself a process that requires practice, patience, and persistence. Like the sales skills you'll be teaching your team, coaching skills must be developed, refined, and continuously improved. The investment you make in becoming a better coach will pay dividends not only in improved sales results but also in the satisfaction that comes from helping others reach their full potential.

The time has come to move beyond traditional management approaches and embrace the transformative power of coaching. Your team is waiting, your Customers are counting on you, and your competition is vulnerable. Let's begin the journey toward **GREAT** sales coaching excellence.

Part 1:

The GREAT Sales Coaching Framework

Chapter 1

The Foundation of Sales Leadership - Why Coaching Matters More Than Management

In the bustling world of retail, where competition is fierce and Customer expectations continue to rise like a soufflé in a hot oven (and can deflate just as quickly if mishandled), one truth remains as constant as the law of gravity: the difference between mediocre and exceptional performance lies not in the products on the shelves, but in the people behind the counter. While retailers scramble to match each other on merchandise selection, pricing, and store ambiance—playing an endless game of retail chess where everyone seems to be copying everyone else's moves—the most successful ones have discovered a secret weapon that their competitors often overlook entirely: their sales team's knowledge, skills, and motivation.

The Retail Reality: People Over Products

This revelation shouldn't surprise us, yet it continues to elude many leaders who remain fixated on operational metrics and inventory turnover rates. It's rather like focusing on the quality of paint while ignoring the skill of the artist—you might have the finest materials in the world, but without capable hands to wield them, you're unlikely to create a masterpiece.

The traditional command-and-control management style that dominated the industrial age made perfect sense when work consisted primarily of repetitive tasks that could be standardized, measured, and optimized. Workers were essentially human machines, expected to follow procedures precisely and consistently. Deviation from established protocols was viewed as problematic, and success was measured primarily through compliance and efficiency metrics.

But here's where things get interesting: retail isn't manufacturing. Unlike factory workers producing identical widgets on an assembly line, retail sales associates deal with an endless variety of human beings, each with unique needs, preferences, communication styles, and decision-making processes. No two Customer interactions are identical, which means no two sales conversations can follow the same script. This variability isn't a bug in the retail system—it's a feature that demands adaptability, creativity, and emotional intelligence from sales professionals.

Consider this curious paradox: the more we try to standardize human interactions, the less human they become. And Customers, being human themselves, can sense artificial or scripted interactions faster than a bloodhound can detect bacon. They want authentic connections, genuine expertise, and personalized solutions to their problems. These qualities can't be mandated through policy—they must be developed through coaching.

The neuroscience behind this distinction is fascinating and provides compelling evidence for why coaching outperforms traditional management approaches. When people feel threatened or criticized—which often happens in command-and-control environments—their brains activate what researchers call the "threat network." This network, centered around the amygdala, essentially hijacks the prefrontal cortex's capacity for learning, creativity, and complex problem-solving.

It's rather like trying to perform brain surgery while someone is shouting at you—technically possible, but far from optimal conditions. The brain's threat response evolved to help our ancestors survive immediate physical dangers, not to navigate complex Customer service situations. When this ancient alarm system activates in modern retail environments, it impairs the very capabilities that excellent Customer service requires.

Conversely, coaching approaches activate what neuroscientists call the "reward network," centered around areas of the brain associated with learning, growth, and positive social connection. When people feel supported and encouraged, their brains release dopamine and other neurochemicals that enhance learning capacity, increase motivation, and improve performance. It's like the difference between trying to garden in drought conditions versus providing optimal water, sunlight, and nutrients—the same seeds that struggle to survive in harsh conditions can flourish when given proper support.

Research Evidence and Competitive Advantages

Research conducted by the Corporate Leadership Council examined over 50,000 employees across various industries and found that companies with effective coaching programs achieve 39% higher employee retention rates and 33% higher revenue growth compared to their peers. These aren't marginal improvements—they represent substantial competitive advantages that compound over time.

But perhaps even more intriguing is what happens to Customer experiences when sales associates receive effective coaching. A study by the Harvard Business Review found that Customers served by coached sales professionals reported 23% higher satisfaction scores and were 31% more likely to make repeat purchases. The ripple effects extend beyond individual transactions to encompass brand loyalty, word-of-mouth marketing, and long-term Customer lifetime value.

The Identity Shift: From Manager to Coach

The transformation from manager to coach requires a fundamental shift in identity and purpose that many leaders find challenging. Managers derive satisfaction from control, efficiency, and problem-solving. Coaches find fulfillment in developing others, facilitating breakthroughs, and creating conditions where people can excel. It's the difference between being the star performer and being the person who helps others become stars.

This identity shift can be particularly challenging for retail leaders who were promoted based on their own sales performance. The skills that made them successful individual contributors—competitive drive, personal accountability, results focus—don't automatically translate into effective coaching capabilities. In fact, some of these qualities can actually hinder coaching effectiveness if not channeled appropriately.

Consider the curious case of Michael Jordan's coaching career. Widely regarded as one of the greatest basketball players of all time, Jordan's brief stint as a coach was notably unsuccessful. His incredibly high personal standards and intense competitive drive, which served him brilliantly as a player, proved counterproductive when working with team members who possessed different capabilities and motivations. The qualities that made him legendary as a performer worked against him as a developer of others.

This pattern appears frequently in retail environments where top sales performers are promoted to management roles without adequate preparation for the coaching responsibilities they'll inherit. They may become frustrated when team members can't immediately replicate their success, leading to micromanagement, impatience, or unrealistic performance expectations that ultimately demoralize rather than inspire.

The most effective sales coaches understand that their role is not to create clones of themselves, but to help each team member discover and develop their own unique strengths and capabilities. This requires a level of emotional intelligence and interpersonal skill that extends far beyond sales technique knowledge.

Cultural considerations also play a significant role in the coaching versus management distinction. In cultures that emphasize hierarchy and authority, team members may initially feel uncomfortable with coaching approaches that involve collaborative goal-setting and two-way feedback. They may interpret coaching behaviors as signs of weakness or uncertainty rather than supportive development activities.

Conversely, in cultures that value individual autonomy and self-direction, team members may resist traditional management approaches that feel controlling or patronizing. Understanding these cultural dynamics and adapting coaching approaches accordingly represents an advanced skill that separates truly effective coaches from those who apply one-size-fits-all methods.

Coaching Can Make You (And Them) Money

The economic implications of coaching versus management extend beyond immediate performance metrics to encompass recruitment, retention, and reputation factors that affect long-term business sustainability. Organizations known for developing their people become magnets for top talent, creating virtuous cycles where excellent people attract other excellent people.

This phenomenon, known as the "talent gravity effect," can provide sustainable competitive advantages that are difficult for competitors to replicate. While products, prices, and marketing strategies can be copied relatively quickly, organizational cultures and coaching capabilities take years to develop and are much harder to duplicate.

The measurement of coaching effectiveness presents unique challenges that distinguish it from traditional management metrics. While management success can often be measured through short-term operational indicators like sales targets, inventory turnover, or cost reduction, coaching success requires longer-term metrics that capture development, engagement, and capability building.

This temporal difference can create tension in organizations focused on quarterly results and immediate performance improvements. Coaching investments may not show immediate returns, but their long-term impact on organizational capability and competitive advantage can be substantial. Leaders who understand this distinction are more likely to maintain coaching commitments even when facing short-term performance pressures.

The technology revolution has created both opportunities and challenges for sales coaching in retail environments. Digital tools can provide unprecedented insights into Customer behavior, sales patterns, and performance metrics that can inform coaching conversations and track development progress. However, technology can also create temptations to rely on data and automation rather than human connection and relationship building.

The most effective modern coaching approaches blend technological capabilities with human insight, using data to **inform** coaching decisions while maintaining focus on the relational and emotional aspects of development that only human coaches can provide. This hybrid approach leverages the best of both worlds while avoiding the pitfalls of either pure technology dependence or purely intuitive coaching methods.

As we look toward the future of retail, several trends suggest that coaching capabilities will become even more critical for organizational success. The continued growth of e-commerce means that physical retail experiences must provide value that online shopping cannot—personalized service, expert consultation, and emotional connection. These qualities require highly developed human skills that can only be cultivated through effective coaching.

Additionally, the increasing pace of change in retail technology, consumer behavior, and competitive dynamics means that organizations must become more adaptable and resilient. These qualities emerge from people who are confident in their ability to learn new skills and adapt to changing circumstances—qualities that effective coaching helps develop.

The journey from management to coaching represents more than a professional development opportunity—it's a chance to fundamentally impact the lives and careers of the people you serve. When done well, coaching doesn't just improve sales performance; it builds confidence, develops capabilities, and creates positive experiences that team members carry with them throughout their careers.

As we prepare to dive deeper into the specific frameworks and techniques that make coaching effective, remember that the foundation of all great coaching is genuine care for the people being developed. Technical knowledge and systematic approaches are important, but they're most powerful when applied with authentic concern for others' success and growth. The combination of care and competence creates coaching relationships that transform not just performance, but lives.

Chapter 2

The GREAT Coaching Framework - Your Five-Step System to Success

If you've ever tried to assemble furniture from a certain Swedish retailer without following the instructions (we've all been there), you'll appreciate why having a systematic framework for coaching is essential. Just as those mysteriously named furniture pieces won't magically transform into a bookshelf without following the proper sequence, effective coaching doesn't happen through good intentions and random acts of development. It requires a proven, step-by-step methodology that ensures consistency, effectiveness, and real results.

The **GREAT** Sales Coaching framework isn't just another acronym dreamed up in a corporate conference room—it represents decades of research in adult learning theory, cognitive psychology, and organizational development, distilled into a practical system that any leader can master. The beauty of this framework lies not in its complexity, but in its elegant simplicity and universal applicability across different personality types, learning styles, and coaching situations.

Let's decode this framework:

- **G**et Ready (Prepare)
- **R**eveal through demonstration (Demonstrate)
- **E**ngage through practice (Have Them Do It)
- **A**ffirm and encourage (Keep It Positive)
- **T**rack progress (Follow Up)

Each letter represents not just a step in the process, but a fundamental principle that addresses specific aspects of how adults learn most effectively.

The sequential nature of the **GREAT** framework isn't arbitrary—it's based on extensive research into how the human brain processes new information and develops new capabilities. Neuroscientists have discovered that learning involves multiple stages: attention and encoding (getting the information into working memory), consolidation (transferring information to long-term memory), and retrieval (accessing stored information for use). The **GREAT** framework aligns perfectly with these natural learning processes.

Consider what happens when we violate this natural sequence. Imagine trying to have someone practice a skill they've never seen demonstrated or attempting to provide feedback before establishing psychological safety. It's like trying to build a house by starting with the roof—technically possible, but inefficient and prone to collapse under pressure.

The framework's universality is particularly fascinating when we examine how it applies across different cultures and contexts. While the specific implementation might vary based on cultural norms or individual preferences, the underlying sequence remains remarkably consistent. This suggests that the **GREAT** framework taps into fundamental human learning processes that transcend cultural boundaries.

Get Ready (Prepare) addresses the critical but often overlooked emotional and psychological prerequisites for effective learning. Adult learners come to coaching situations carrying invisible backpacks filled with past experiences, current anxieties, and future concerns that can either facilitate or hinder their development. The preparation phase is where skilled coaches help learners unpack these psychological barriers and create optimal conditions for growth.

Research in educational psychology has consistently demonstrated that learner readiness accounts for up to 40% of learning effectiveness—more than teaching method or content quality. This finding should give pause to any coach tempted to skip preparation in favor of getting straight to skill development. The time invested in proper preparation typically reduces total coaching time by making subsequent phases more efficient and effective.

The neuroscience behind preparation is particularly compelling. When people feel anxious or threatened, their brains activate what researchers call the "default mode network"—a system that prioritizes threat detection over learning and creativity. Effective preparation helps shift brain activity toward the "task-positive network," which enhances focus, memory consolidation, and skill acquisition.

Reveal through demonstration (Demonstrate) leverages the power of observational learning, a fundamental human capability that enabled our species to develop complex cultures and technologies. Mirror neurons—specialized brain cells that activate both when performing an action and when observing others perform the same action—provide the biological foundation for learning through demonstration.

However, effective demonstration is far more sophisticated than simply "showing someone how it's done." It requires deliberate skill breakdown, thoughtful sequencing, and careful attention to the observer's cognitive capacity and learning preferences. The best demonstrators function like skilled directors, managing multiple elements simultaneously to create learning experiences that are both comprehensive and digestible.

Interestingly, research has shown that demonstrations including intentional errors followed by corrections are often more effective than perfect demonstrations. This "productive failure" approach helps learners understand not just what to do, but what not to do and how to recover when things don't go as planned. It's rather like learning to drive by observing both excellent driving and common mistakes—you develop a more complete understanding of the skill.

Engage through practice (Have Them Do It) transforms passive observation into active capability building. This phase recognizes that adults learn best through experiential practice rather than passive absorption of information. The old Chinese proverb captures this beautifully: "Tell me and I forget, teach me and I may remember, involve me and I learn."

The challenge lies in designing practice experiences that are challenging enough to promote growth but not so difficult that they overwhelm or discourage learners. Sports psychology research has identified this sweet spot as the "optimal challenge zone"—a state where skills are stretched but not broken, where learners feel energized rather than exhausted by their efforts.

Modern neuroscience has revealed fascinating insights about how practice creates lasting behavioral change. Each time we practice a skill, we strengthen the neural pathways associated with that behavior while simultaneously weakening competing pathways. This process, called "synaptic plasticity," explains why consistent practice is more effective than sporadic intensive training sessions.

Affirm and encourage (Keep It Positive) harnesses the power of positive psychology to maintain motivation and accelerate learning. This isn't about superficial cheerleading or avoiding necessary corrections—it's about creating emotional conditions that optimize brain function and promote resilience in the face of challenges.

The research on positive reinforcement is both extensive and compelling. Studies have shown that the optimal ratio of positive to corrective feedback is approximately 5:1 for high-performing teams and 3:1 for average teams. This doesn't mean avoiding difficult conversations or "speaking the truth in love" but rather ensuring that developmental feedback occurs within a context of recognition and support.

What's particularly intriguing is how positive reinforcement affects not just motivation, but actual learning capacity. When people receive genuine recognition for their efforts and progress, their brains release dopamine—a neurotransmitter that enhances memory consolidation and increases motivation for continued learning. It's like adding high-octane fuel to the learning engine.

Track progress (Follow Up) ensures that coaching creates lasting behavioral change rather than temporary performance fluctuations. This phase recognizes that skill development is a process that extends well beyond formal coaching sessions and requires ongoing support, monitoring, and adjustment.

The science of habit formation reveals why follow-up is so crucial. New behaviors exist in a fragile state for weeks or months after initial learning, competing with established habits and patterns that have been reinforced over years. Without systematic follow-up, even well-learned skills can deteriorate under pressure or competing priorities.

Research by the European Journal of Social Psychology found that it takes an average of 66 days for new behaviors to become automatic, with significant variation based on complexity and individual differences. I've always thought of it as two months since that is easier to remember. This finding has profound implications for coaching programs—effective follow-up must extend for months, not days or weeks.

One Size Does Not Fit All

The framework's adaptability represents one of its greatest strengths. While the five steps remain constant, how they're implemented can be customized for different learning styles, personality types, cultural backgrounds, and skill levels. A visual learner might benefit from diagrams and flowcharts during demonstration, while a kinesthetic learner needs more hands-on practice opportunities. The framework provides structure while maintaining flexibility.

This customization capability becomes particularly important when coaching diverse teams that include multiple generations, cultural backgrounds, and experience levels. A framework that works for everyone while being customizable for anyone represents the ideal balance between consistency and personalization.

The economic implications of using a systematic coaching framework extend far beyond individual skill development. Organizations that implement structured coaching approaches report higher employee engagement, reduced turnover, improved Customer satisfaction, and increased profitability. A study by the International Coach Federation found that companies with strong coaching cultures report 21% higher profitability than their peers.

These results aren't accidental—they reflect the compound effects of systematic capability building across entire organizations. When every manager uses the same high-quality coaching approach, it creates consistency in development experiences and accelerates organizational learning.

The framework also addresses one of the most common coaching failures: inconsistency. Without a systematic approach, even well-intentioned coaches can fall into patterns of playing favorites, focusing disproportionately on weaknesses while ignoring strengths, or providing feedback that confuses rather than clarifies. The **GREAT** framework serves as a quality control mechanism that ensures all team members receive effective development support.

Technology integration with the **GREAT** framework opens exciting possibilities for enhancing coaching effectiveness while maintaining human connection. Learning management systems can track progress through each phase, video platforms can enhance demonstration capabilities, mobile apps can provide practice opportunities, and analytics can identify patterns that inform coaching improvements.

However, technology should amplify rather than replace human judgment and relationship building. The most effective modern coaching approaches blend technological capabilities with emotional intelligence, using data to inform decisions while maintaining focus on the human elements that make coaching transformational.

It's Not About You

The scalability of the **GREAT** Sales Coaching framework makes it particularly valuable for growing organizations. Unlike coaching approaches that depend heavily on individual coach talent or charisma, the **GREAT** framework can be taught, measured, and replicated across large numbers of leaders. This scalability enables organizations to maintain coaching quality as they expand.

Common implementation pitfalls include rushing through the preparation phase to get to "real" coaching, providing demonstrations that are too complex or fast-paced, allowing practice sessions to become performance evaluations, giving feedback that focuses more on problems than progress, and failing to provide adequate follow-up support.

Understanding these pitfalls helps coaches avoid them, but more importantly, it highlights why each phase of the framework is essential. Attempting to shortcut any phase typically results in longer total coaching time and less effective outcomes.

The framework's effectiveness can be measured through both leading indicators (participation rates, engagement levels, skill demonstration in practice) and lagging indicators (performance improvements, retention rates, Customer satisfaction). This measurement capability enables continuous improvement of coaching methods and provides data to justify coaching investments.

Advanced practitioners of the **GREAT** framework often develop sophisticated variations that address specific coaching challenges or opportunities. These might include specialized preparation techniques for resistant learners, advanced demonstration methods for complex skills, practice designs that simulate high-pressure situations, positive reinforcement strategies for different personality types, or follow-up approaches for various career development stages.

The framework's longevity and continued relevance in rapidly changing business environments stem from its foundation in fundamental human learning processes rather than specific techniques or technologies. While the tools and contexts of coaching may evolve, the basic sequence of preparing learners, demonstrating skills, facilitating practice, maintaining motivation, and ensuring application remains constant.

Cultural translation of the **GREAT** framework requires sensitivity to different values, communication styles, and learning preferences while maintaining the essential elements that make it effective. In hierarchical cultures, the preparation phase might need to address respect and authority concerns. In individualistic cultures, the positive reinforcement phase might emphasize personal achievement rather than group contributions.

The framework's impact on organizational culture extends beyond individual coaching relationships to influence how people throughout the organization approach learning and development. When the **GREAT** Sales Coaching approach becomes normalized, it creates environments where continuous improvement is expected rather than exceptional.

Quality assurance in **GREAT** framework implementation requires ongoing attention to coach development, feedback systems, and outcome measurement. Organizations that achieve the best results invest in coach training, provide coaching supervision, and continuously refine their approaches based on results and feedback.

The future evolution of the **GREAT** framework will likely incorporate advances in neuroscience, artificial intelligence, and personalized learning technologies while maintaining its core focus on human development and relationship building. As our understanding of how people learn and grow continues to advance, the framework will undoubtedly be refined and enhanced while preserving the essential elements that make it effective.

The **GREAT** Sales Coaching framework represents more than just a methodology—it embodies a philosophy that believes in human potential and provides a practical roadmap for unlocking that potential. When implemented with skill, commitment, and genuine care for others' development, it becomes a powerful engine for individual growth and organizational transformation.

Chapter 3

Get Ready (Prepare) - Setting the Stage for Learning Excellence

Picture this: you're about to perform in a concert, but instead of walking onto a well-lit stage with a tuned instrument and an engaged audience, you find yourself in a dimly lit room with a broken guitar and a crowd of people checking their phones. The music might be beautiful, but the conditions for success are so poor that even Mozart would struggle to create a memorable performance. This scenario perfectly illustrates why the Prepare phase of coaching is so crucial—it's where we create the conditions that make beautiful learning music possible.

The G in **GREAT** Sales Coaching is *Get Ready (Prepare)*. It is in this Prepare phase where coaching magic truly begins, yet it's often the most undervalued and rushed component of the development process. Like a master chef who spends hours preparing ingredients before the actual cooking begins, skilled coaches understand that the quality of preparation directly determines the success of everything that follows. Rush the prep work, and even the most sophisticated coaching techniques will fall flat.

The Psychology of Adult Learning and Mental Barriers

The psychology of adult learning reveals why preparation is so critical. Unlike children, who often approach new experiences with natural curiosity and minimal preconceptions, adults enter learning situations carrying sophisticated mental models about themselves, their capabilities, and their experiences with previous training or coaching attempts. These mental models can either facilitate learning or create nearly insurmountable barriers to growth.

Consider the fascinating research conducted by Stanford psychologist Claude Steele on "stereotype threat"—the phenomenon where people's performance decreases when they're aware of negative stereotypes about their group. In coaching contexts, this might manifest as older employees worrying about their ability to learn new technologies, experienced salespeople feeling threatened by suggestions that their current methods need improvement, or introverted team members becoming anxious about role-playing exercises.

The **Get Ready** phase is specifically designed to address these psychological barriers before they can interfere with skill development. It's like clearing the static from a radio signal—once the interference is removed, the message comes through clearly and powerfully.

Neuroscientist Dr. Matthew Lieberman's research at UCLA has revealed fascinating insights about how the brain responds to learning situations. When people feel socially threatened or judged, the anterior cingulate cortex (the brain's alarm system) becomes hyperactive, essentially hijacking cognitive resources needed for learning and memory formation. Conversely, when people feel supported and valued, the brain's reward networks activate, releasing neurochemicals that enhance learning capacity and motivation. Put a simpler way, if we are worried about what people think about us (the coach) then we expend our energy on worry versus learning.

This neurological reality explains why traditional "sink or swim" training approaches are so ineffective. They activate the very brain systems that inhibit learning while suppressing those that facilitate it. Effective preparation does the opposite—it calms the threat response while activating reward and learning networks.

Creating Psychological Safety and Building Trust

The first element of masterful preparation is creating what Harvard Business School professor Amy Edmondson calls "psychological safety"—the belief that one can show vulnerability, ask questions, and make mistakes without fear of negative consequences. This isn't about lowering standards or avoiding difficult conversations; it's about creating environments where people feel safe to be learners rather than feeling pressured to appear knowledgeable.

Psychological safety is built through a combination of explicit communication and implicit behavior. Explicitly, coaches can establish ground rules that normalize learning struggles, emphasize growth over perfection, and create agreements about confidentiality and respect. Implicitly, coaches build safety through their tone of voice, body language, listening behavior, and responses to questions or mistakes.

One of the most powerful techniques for building psychological safety is vulnerability modeling—where coaches share their own learning experiences, including challenges they've faced and mistakes they've made. Fortunately for me (unfortunately for my past managers who had to deal with me) I have had lots of poor experiences to draw from. This approach serves multiple purposes: it humanizes you as the coach, normalizes the learning process, and demonstrates that even experienced professionals continue to grow and develop.

For example, a coach might say: "When I first started learning these Customer research techniques, I was so focused on asking the 'right' questions that I forgot to listen to the answers. I remember one interaction where I asked the same question three different ways because I wasn't paying attention to what the Customer was telling me. Let me share what I learned from that experience..." (Yes, that is not simply an example, but my real life in play!)

This type of sharing immediately reduces the pressure to be perfect and helps learners understand that struggling with new skills is normal and expected rather than a sign of incompetence or failure.

Understanding Individual Motivations

The second critical element of preparation involves understanding and addressing individual motivations and concerns. Adults are motivated to learn when they can clearly see how new skills or knowledge will benefit them personally. This means going beyond generic statements about improving performance to identify specific, relevant benefits that resonate with each individual's unique situation and goals.

Some team members might be motivated by the prospect of increased confidence in Customer interactions. Others might be drawn to the potential for higher commissions or career advancement opportunities. Still others might be inspired by the challenge of mastering new skills or the opportunity to provide better Customer service. Effective coaches invest time in discovering what motivates each team member and frame coaching experiences in terms of those specific motivations.

This individualized approach requires skilled questioning and careful listening. Coaches might ask questions like: "What aspects of Customer interactions do you find most challenging?" "What would success look like for you in this area?" "How do you think these skills might impact your work or career?" The answers to these questions provide valuable insights that can be used to customize the entire coaching experience.

Cultural sensitivity plays an increasingly important role in preparation as retail teams become more diverse. Different cultural backgrounds can significantly influence how people respond to coaching, feedback, and learning activities. Some cultures emphasize collective harmony and might be uncomfortable with individual recognition or competition. Others prioritize respect for authority and might initially resist collaborative coaching approaches that seem to diminish traditional hierarchy.

Effective coaches develop cultural intelligence—the ability to understand and adapt to different cultural perspectives while maintaining the essential elements of effective coaching. This doesn't mean stereotyping or making assumptions, but rather remaining sensitive to cultural differences and adjusting approaches when necessary.

The timing and environment of preparation conversations significantly impact their effectiveness. These discussions should occur when both coach and team member can focus without distractions, and they should take place in settings that feel comfortable and private rather than intimidating or public. The physical environment sends powerful messages about the nature and importance of the coaching relationship.

Attention to details like seating arrangements (chairs at angles rather than across a desk), lighting (warm and welcoming rather than harsh), and interruptions (phones silenced, doors closed) can dramatically impact the quality of preparation conversations. These elements might seem minor, but they collectively communicate respect, professionalism, and commitment to the team member's development.

One of the most common mistakes in preparation is rushing through it to get to the "real" coaching. This impatience is understandable—leaders are busy, and there's often pressure to see immediate results. However, time invested in thorough preparation typically reduces total coaching time by eliminating resistance, increasing engagement, and accelerating skill acquisition.

Think of preparation like foundation work in construction. While it might seem like time that could be better spent on visible building activities, cutting corners on foundation work inevitably leads to problems that are much more expensive and time-consuming to fix later. The same principle applies to coaching preparation.

The **Get Ready** (Prepare) phase also includes setting up the specific learning context and addressing common concerns about the coaching process itself. Many adults have negative associations with training or coaching based on past experiences with poorly designed or executed programs. These negative associations can create resistance that undermines even well-designed coaching efforts.

Effective coaches proactively address these concerns by explaining their coaching philosophy, describing what team members can expect during the process, and establishing clear agreements about goals, expectations, and mutual responsibilities. This upfront clarification prevents many misunderstandings and helps build confidence in the coaching process.

No Train No Gain

Role-playing, which features prominently in sales coaching, often requires special attention during preparation because many people have negative associations with practice exercises based on forced, artificial, or embarrassing past experiences. Reframing role-play as "rehearsal," "practice," or "skill refinement" can help overcome these negative associations while emphasizing the professional development aspects of the activities.

The conversation might sound like this: "I know some people feel awkward about role-playing, and that's completely normal. Think of this like musicians rehearsing before a concert or athletes practicing before a game. We're going to create a safe space where you can try new techniques, get feedback, and refine your approach before using these skills with Customers. The goal isn't perfect performance—it's improvement and confidence building."

Confidence Building and Long-Term Impact

Confidence building represents another crucial aspect of preparation. Rather than immediately focusing on skill gaps or performance issues, effective coaches begin by acknowledging existing strengths and positive behaviors. This approach, based on appreciative inquiry principles, creates a foundation of confidence that supports risk-taking and experimentation during the learning process.

The conversation might begin with observations like: "I've noticed that Customers respond really well to your friendly greeting and your genuine interest in helping them find what they need. Those are fundamental strengths that we'll build on as we work on some additional techniques that can help you be even more effective."

This strength-based framing positions coaching as enhancement rather than remediation, which significantly impacts how the experience is perceived and internalized. Team members who feel appreciated for their existing contributions are much more likely to be open to suggestions for improvement.

Technology can enhance preparation when used thoughtfully and appropriately. Pre-coaching assessments delivered through mobile apps or online platforms can help team members reflect on their current skills and goals before coaching conversations begin. Video platforms can provide opportunities for team members to observe excellent Customer interactions before their own coaching sessions.

However, technology should supplement rather than replace human connection during preparation. The relationship between coach and team member is the foundation upon which all other coaching activities rest, and this relationship is built through personal interaction, genuine conversation, and mutual respect.

The duration and depth of preparation should be customized based on individual needs and circumstances. The **Get Ready** phase for new team members typically requires more extensive preparation as they adjust to new roles, organizational culture, and performance expectations. Experienced team members might need less preparation time but may require different approaches that acknowledge their expertise while introducing new concepts.

Resistant or skeptical team members often need additional preparation time to address their concerns and build buy-in for the coaching process. This might involve multiple conversations, gradual introduction to coaching concepts, or demonstration of coaching value through small initial successes.

Advanced preparation techniques include stakeholder mapping (identifying other people who influence the team member's success), barrier analysis (systematically identifying potential obstacles to learning), and success visualization (helping team members imagine themselves successfully applying new skills).

The measurement of preparation effectiveness can include indicators such as team member engagement during subsequent coaching phases, willingness to participate in practice activities, quality of questions asked during coaching sessions, and speed of skill acquisition. These metrics help coaches refine their preparation approaches and identify team members who might need additional support.

Be Careful Not To Assume

Common preparation pitfalls include making assumptions about team member motivations, rushing through psychological safety building, failing to address cultural differences, inadequate attention to physical environment, and insufficient time allocation for thorough preparation conversations.

The long-term impact of thorough preparation extends far beyond individual coaching sessions to influence team member attitudes toward continuous learning, willingness to seek help when needed, and openness to feedback and development throughout their careers. Team members who experience respectful, thorough preparation are more likely to become advocates for coaching and development within their organizations.

Quality preparation also demonstrates the coach's commitment to the team member's success, which builds trust and credibility that enhance all subsequent coaching interactions. When team members feel that their coach has invested genuine time and effort in understanding their needs and creating optimal learning conditions, they're much more likely to invest their own effort in the development process.

The **Get Ready** (Prepare) phase concludes with clear agreements about the coaching journey ahead, including logistics like scheduling and time commitments, but more importantly, mutual understanding about goals, expectations, and the collaborative nature of the learning relationship. When preparation is done well, team members leave these conversations feeling excited rather than anxious about their development opportunity.

The mastery of preparation requires patience, empathy, and genuine respect for the people being coached. It demands that coaches set aside their own agenda and timeline to focus on creating optimal conditions for each individual's learning and development. This investment in preparation transforms coaching from something that happens to team members into something they actively participate in, value, and ultimately own.

Chapter 4

Reveal Through Demonstration (Demonstrate) - The Art of Showing the Way

If you've ever tried to assemble something complex by reading instructions alone—say, a barbecue grill or a child's bicycle—you'll appreciate the transformative power of watching someone else do it first. Suddenly, those confusing diagrams and cryptic instructions become crystal clear when you can observe the actual process in action. This same phenomenon explains why demonstration is such a powerful component of the **GREAT** Sales Coaching framework, yet like many powerful tools, its effectiveness depends entirely on how skillfully it's wielded.

In Phase 2 of the **GREAT** Framework, *Reveal Through Demonstration (Demonstrate)*, we see that the art of demonstration goes far beyond simply "showing someone how it's done." It requires the sophisticated ability to make the invisible visible, to break down complex behaviors into learnable components, and to create mental templates that learners can internalize and adapt to their own situations. Master demonstrators function like skilled directors of learning, managing multiple elements simultaneously to create experiences that are both comprehensive and digestible.

The Science Behind Effective Demonstration

The scientific foundation for demonstration's effectiveness lies in what neuroscientists call "mirror neurons"—specialized brain cells that fire both when we perform an action and when we observe others performing the same action. These remarkable cells, discovered somewhat accidentally by Italian researcher Giacomo Rizzolatti while studying macaque monkeys, provide the neurological basis for learning through imitation.

But here's where it gets really interesting: mirror neurons don't just copy what they observe—they also activate the observer's motor cortex, creating what researchers describe as "embodied simulation." When you watch someone demonstrate a sales technique, your brain actually rehearses performing that technique, laying down neural pathways that facilitate your own performance when the time comes to practice. Now that's cool.

This neurological reality has profound implications for how demonstrations should be structured and delivered. Simply performing a skill naturally, while better than not demonstrating at all, fails to leverage the full potential of mirror neuron systems. Effective demonstrations require deliberate slowing down, explicit narration of decision-making processes, and careful attention to what the observer's brain needs to create useful internal models.

Deliberate Practice and What They Can Handle

The challenge of effective demonstration becomes apparent when we consider the complexity of even seemingly simple Customer interactions. What appears to be a straightforward greeting involves dozens of micro-decisions: when to make eye contact, how to modulate tone of voice, what words to emphasize, how to position one's body, when to smile, how long to maintain silence for Customer responses, and countless other elements that experienced professionals execute unconsciously.

This unconscious competence, while valuable for performance, becomes a barrier to teaching others. The most skilled sales professionals often struggle as demonstrators because they've automated so many behaviors that they're no longer aware of what they're doing or why they're doing it. Effective coaching demonstrations require conscious competence—the ability to perform skills deliberately while maintaining awareness of all the components involved.

The concept of "deliberate practice," developed through K. Anders Ericsson's research on expert performance, provides crucial insights for designing effective demonstrations. Rather than simply performing skills naturally, deliberate practice requires breaking down complex behaviors into component parts, performing each part with focused attention, and providing explicit feedback about performance quality.

When applied to demonstrations, this means slowing down natural performance, highlighting specific techniques being employed, and providing running commentary about decision-making processes. For example, instead of simply greeting a role-play Customer naturally, an effective demonstrator might say: "Notice how I'm making eye contact before speaking—this creates an immediate connection. Now I'll use a warm tone of voice and include their name to personalize the greeting. I'm also going to mention something specific about our store to begin building brand awareness right from the first moment."

This type of explicit narration serves multiple purposes: it makes unconscious behaviors conscious, provides rationale for specific choices, demonstrates how techniques can be adapted to different situations, and helps observers understand the thinking behind effective performance rather than just the actions themselves.

The sequencing of demonstration components requires careful consideration of cognitive load theory, which suggests that people can only process limited amounts of new information simultaneously. Attempting to demonstrate entire sales processes in single sessions often results in cognitive overload, where observers become overwhelmed and retain little useful information.

Instead, effective demonstrations focus on specific skills or techniques at a time, ensuring comprehension before moving to additional components. This might mean dedicating one demonstration session to greeting techniques, another to questioning strategies, and a third to closing methods. While this approach requires more total demonstration time, it results in much better learning outcomes.

This is one I have learned through the years - especially when doing sales coaching - you should never try and do the entire sales process at once. In fact, focus on one skill of the process each session. You can progressively add more as you build but never add to the roleplay or demonstration until you know they have mastered the skill you are working on.

Creating Positive Learning Environments

The emotional climate during demonstrations significantly impacts their effectiveness. Observers who feel judged or pressured often focus more on their own anxiety than on the techniques being shown. Conversely, when the atmosphere feels supportive and encouraging, observers can fully engage with the learning content.

Creating positive demonstration environments requires attention to both explicit and implicit communication. Explicitly, demonstrators can emphasize learning over evaluation, normalize mistakes and adjustments, and encourage questions throughout the process. Implicitly, positive environments are created through tone of voice, body language, facial expressions, and energy levels that convey enthusiasm rather than obligation.

One particularly powerful technique is the use of intentional imperfection followed by correction. This approach, sometimes called "productive failure," involves deliberately making errors during demonstrations and then showing how to recover or improve. This technique serves multiple purposes: it normalizes mistake-making, demonstrates problem-solving processes, shows that even experts continue learning, and provides realistic examples of how to handle common challenges. And for many learners, it's just fine. And we need to add some fun to the coaching process to make it more engaging.

For example, a demonstrator might role-play a Customer interaction where they initially ask a closed-ended question, then pause and say: "Let me try that again with an open-ended question that will give me more useful information about what they're looking for." This approach reduces performance pressure on observers while providing practical examples of self-correction and improvement.

Leveraging Peer Demonstrations and Technology

The use of multiple demonstrators can significantly enhance learning experiences when managed appropriately. While the coach should typically provide initial demonstrations to ensure accuracy and consistency, having successful team members also demonstrate techniques offers several advantages: it shows that techniques can be adapted to different personality styles, provides recognition and development opportunities for high performers, creates more peer-to-peer learning opportunities, and demonstrates that skills are achievable by "regular people" rather than just expert coaches.

And let's be honest, they tend to listen more to their peers than they do to you. Plus, you are not trying to build a team full of human AI robots. You are teaching principles. You want each person to infuse his or her own personality into the sales process to make it more genuine. Using peers really demonstrates this point well.

However, peer demonstrations require careful management to maintain quality and consistency. This involves clear guidelines about what should be demonstrated, constructive feedback when corrections are needed, and follow-up coaching for team members who serve as demonstrators. The goal is leveraging peer modeling while maintaining coaching standards.

Technology can enhance demonstrations when used appropriately and thoughtfully. High-quality video recordings of excellent Customer interactions (with proper permissions and privacy protections) can provide examples of techniques in action with real Customers. These recordings offer unique advantages: they can be paused for discussion, replayed for analysis, and reviewed individually by team members who need additional reinforcement.

Virtual reality systems, while still emerging in retail training applications, offer fascinating possibilities for immersive demonstration experiences. VR can create consistent demonstration environments, allow observers to view interactions from multiple perspectives (Customer viewpoint, third-person observer, etc.), and provide repeated access to identical demonstration scenarios.

However, technology should enhance and NEVER replace live human demonstrations. There's something uniquely powerful about observing techniques performed by someone you know and respect, in real-time, with the ability to ask questions and request clarification. The energy, authenticity, and adaptability of live demonstrations create learning experiences that recorded media cannot fully replicate. Plus, when someone sees it on a video or online, they tend to discount what they are seeing thinking "this is so easy when it's not real."

Adapting for Learning Styles and Cultural Considerations

The customization of demonstrations for different learning styles requires understanding how visual, auditory, and kinesthetic learners process information differently. Visual learners benefit from demonstrations that include diagrams, flowcharts, or written reminders that reinforce verbal techniques. Auditory learners need rich verbal explanation, discussion of reasoning behind techniques, and opportunities to ask questions about what they're observing. Kinesthetic learners benefit from demonstrations that emphasize body language, spatial relationships, and physical aspects of Customer interactions.

Effective demonstrators learn to engage multiple learning modalities simultaneously, narrating their actions for auditory learners while maintaining visual clarity for visual learners and emphasizing physical positioning for kinesthetic learners. This multi-modal approach ensures that all team members can access the demonstration content through their preferred learning channels.

Cultural considerations become particularly important when demonstrating interpersonal skills like Customer service techniques. Communication styles that work well with one Customer demographic might be less effective with others, and demonstrators need to address these variations explicitly. This might involve showing how to adapt communication approaches for different age groups, cultural backgrounds, or Customer personality types.

Demonstration Structure and Advanced Techniques

The pacing of demonstrations requires balancing comprehensiveness with engagement. Demonstrations that are too lengthy or detailed can lose the audience's attention, while those that are too brief may leave important questions unanswered. Most effective demonstrations last between 5-15 minutes for specific techniques, with opportunities for questions and discussion throughout rather than only at the end.

Advanced demonstration techniques can address specific learning objectives and challenge more experienced team members. These might include handling difficult Customer situations, managing multiple Customers simultaneously, dealing with technical questions beyond one's expertise, or navigating complex product comparisons with budget-conscious Customers.

The integration of storytelling with demonstrations can significantly enhance their impact and memorability. Rather than presenting techniques in isolation, effective demonstrators embed skills within realistic scenarios that observers can relate to their own experiences. These scenarios might be based on actual Customer interactions, common challenging situations, or aspirational examples of exceptional service.

For example, instead of simply demonstrating questioning techniques, a skilled demonstrator might create a scenario: "Let me show you how I helped a Customer last week who came in looking for a drill but actually needed a solution for hanging heavy pictures in their apartment. Notice how the questions I ask help us discover what they're really trying to accomplish..."

The conclusion of demonstration sessions should include clear transitions to practice phases, summaries of key techniques observed, opportunities for clarification questions, and establishment of expectations for upcoming skill practice. Team members should leave demonstrations feeling confident about what they observed and motivated to try the techniques themselves.

Common demonstration pitfalls include performing too quickly for observers to process, failing to explain the reasoning behind specific choices, not adapting to different learning styles, inadequate attention to emotional climate, and insufficient connection between demonstrated techniques and real-world applications.

Measuring Success and Long-term Impact

The measurement of demonstration effectiveness can include observer engagement levels, quality of questions asked during or after demonstrations, retention of demonstrated techniques in subsequent practice sessions, and successful application of techniques in real Customer interactions. These metrics help coaches refine their demonstration approaches and identify areas for improvement.

The long-term impact of skillful demonstrations extends beyond immediate skill transfer to influence team members' mental models of excellence and professionalism. When team members observe high-quality techniques consistently demonstrated with enthusiasm and expertise, it raises their standards and expectations for their own performance.

Master demonstrators understand that they're not just showing techniques—they're modeling attitudes, values, and approaches to Customer service that team members will internalize and carry forward throughout their careers. This responsibility requires demonstrators to consistently exhibit the highest levels of professionalism, authenticity, and commitment to excellence.

The development of demonstration skills represents a crucial competency for sales coaches and requires ongoing practice and refinement. Like the skills being demonstrated, demonstration ability improves through deliberate practice, feedback, and continuous learning. Coaches who commit to mastering the art of demonstration create learning experiences that are both memorable and transformational.

When done with skill and intention, the **Reveal Through Demonstration** (Demonstrate) phase of the **GREAT** framework provides team members with clear mental templates of excellence that guide their own performance development. These internal models become reference points that team members can access during challenging Customer interactions, providing both confidence and direction when they might otherwise feel uncertain about how to proceed.

Chapter 5

Engage Through Practice (Have Them Do It) - Active Learning Through Practice

There's a reason why we don't learn to ride bicycles by reading instruction manuals or watching YouTube videos (though many of us have certainly tried). At some point, we must get on the bike, wobble around embarrassingly, probably fall a few times, and gradually develop the muscle memory and confidence that comes only through actual practice. The same principle applies to sales skills, yet many coaching programs spend 90% of their time on explanation and demonstration, leaving precious little time for the active practice that creates competence.

The third phase of the **GREAT** Sales Coaching framework is *Engage Through Practice* or *Have Them Do It*. This phase represents the crucial transition from knowledge to capability, from understanding to mastery, from knowing what to do to actually being able to do it under pressure. This transition is where coaching separates itself from mere training or information sharing—it's where theory meets reality and potential becomes performance.

The Science of Practice-Based Learning

The scientific foundation for practice-based learning is both extensive and compelling. Hermann Ebbinghaus's pioneering research on memory and forgetting revealed that we lose approximately 50% of new information within the first hour after learning it - the first hour! And up to 90% within a week, unless that information is actively practiced and reinforced. More recent neuroscience research has shown that skills become truly automatic only after approximately 10,000 repetitions—a finding that underscores why one-time training sessions, no matter how well-designed, simply cannot create lasting behavior change.

But here's what makes this phase particularly fascinating: the brain doesn't distinguish between real and simulated practice when it comes to building neural pathways. This means that well-designed role-play scenarios can be nearly as effective as real Customer interactions for developing skills—and often more effective because they can be controlled, repeated, and adjusted based on learning needs.

Overcoming Practice Barriers and Creating Learning Zones

The challenge lies in creating practice experiences that feel authentic and meaningful rather than artificial and embarrassing. This requires understanding the psychological barriers that often make practice feel uncomfortable and developing techniques to overcome those barriers while maintaining learning effectiveness.

One of the most significant barriers to effective practice is what psychologists call "evaluation apprehension"—the anxiety that comes from being observed and potentially judged by others. When people feel they're being evaluated rather than supported, their performance often deteriorates, creating negative practice experiences that can actually harm rather than help skill development.

Let's face it, no one loves roleplay. They may do it, but they usually hate it. Here is the deal. Do you know why your employees say it's so much easier with an actual Customer versus in front of their peers in a roleplay coaching environment?

Because the Customer does not know that what they just did in the role play sucks!

Your peers know you did bad. They know you do not know what you are doing. There is no way to hide it. So, they make excuses hoping you will buy into their nonsense and cancel the role play.

Role-play is hard. No doubt. It *is* much harder than when you are with a Customer—by design. But it is the best way for you to accomplish two very important goals. First, this phase in our process uses role play as a way to live out the Principle of Exercise in learning which states "the more you do it, the better you learn." Second, you get to check for comprehension. Do they really understand? Typically, a trainer or coach will check for comprehension by asking "any questions?" And, of course, there are none. So obviously they all got it. No worries.

Effective practice sessions create what researchers call "learning zones"—psychological spaces where challenge levels are high enough to promote growth but not so high that they trigger anxiety or overwhelm. Creating these zones requires careful calibration of difficulty levels, emotional support, and feedback timing.

Structuring Effective Practice Sessions

The structure of practice sessions should follow what educational psychologists call "progressive complexity"—starting with simplified scenarios that allow learners to focus on basic techniques, then gradually introducing more realistic challenges as confidence and competence develop. This might mean beginning with very cooperative role-play Customers who respond positively to all techniques, then progressively introducing more realistic Customer behaviors including mild objections, time constraints, or specific product requests.

This progressive approach aligns with Vygotsky's concept of the "zone of proximal development"—the difference between what learners can do independently and what they can accomplish with appropriate support. Practice sessions should consistently operate within this zone, providing enough challenge to stretch capabilities while offering sufficient support to ensure success.

The timing and frequency of practice sessions significantly impact their effectiveness. Research on skill acquisition suggests that multiple shorter sessions distributed over time are generally more effective than fewer longer sessions. This "spacing effect" occurs because the brain needs time to consolidate new learning between practice sessions, and distributed practice allows for multiple consolidation cycles.

For sales coaching, this might mean scheduling 15-20 minute practice sessions several times per week rather than one lengthy monthly session. While this approach requires more coordination and time management, it typically results in much faster skill development and better retention.

The role of the coach during practice sessions is complex and demanding. Coaches must simultaneously observe performance, provide realistic Customer responses, monitor emotional state, identify teachable moments, and prepare feedback for delivery after the practice concludes. This multitasking requires high levels of concentration and skill, which is why effective practice coaching is typically conducted one-on-one rather than in large groups.

The quality of "Customer" responses during role-play significantly impacts practice effectiveness. Coaches who play Customers should create consistent, believable characters with specific needs, personalities, and communication styles. These characters should be challenging enough to provide realistic practice opportunities but not so difficult that they discourage learners or prevent skill application.

Developing a repertoire of Customer personas allows coaches to provide variety in practice scenarios while maintaining consistency within individual sessions. A hurried business Customer requires different sales approaches than a leisurely browser and practicing with diverse Customer types builds adaptability and confidence.

Feedback, Peer Practice, and Technology Integration

The feedback delivery process during practice sessions requires careful attention to timing and approach. While it might seem natural to provide corrections immediately upon observing mistakes, research suggests that allowing practice to continue uninterrupted often produces better learning outcomes. Interrupting practice to provide feedback can disrupt the flow of learning and prevent learners from developing self-correction abilities.

Instead, effective coaches typically allow role-play practice scenarios to reach natural completion points before discussing what went well and what could be improved. This approach respects the learning process and allows team members to experience the full context of their performance before receiving feedback.

When feedback is provided, it should be specific rather than general, focusing on particular behaviors rather than overall impressions. Instead of saying "that was good" or "you need to work on your approach," effective coaches provide targeted observations like "Your use of the Customer's name created immediate personal connection, and your follow-up question about their specific needs showed genuine interest in helping them."

The concept of "errorless role-play learning" provides valuable insights for structuring these sessions. This approach suggests that practice should be designed to maximize success experiences while still providing appropriate challenges. This doesn't mean making practice unrealistically easy but rather ensuring that learners experience enough success to build confidence while being stretched enough to promote growth.

Success breeds confidence, and confidence enables risk-taking and experimentation—both essential elements of effective learning. Team members who experience early success in role-play practice are more likely to persist through challenges and continue applying new skills in real Customer interactions.

The emotional journey during role-play sessions often follows predictable patterns: initial nervousness, gradual engagement as focus shifts to the scenario, occasional frustration when techniques don't work as expected, breakthrough moments of understanding, and finally, eagerness to try skills with actual Customers. Understanding this emotional progression helps coaches provide appropriate support at each stage.

Peer practice sessions, when managed skillfully, can add valuable dimensions to the learning experience. Team members practicing with each other can provide different perspectives, learn from various approaches, and create supportive learning communities. However, peer practice requires clear guidelines, skilled facilitation, and careful attention to group dynamics to ensure positive outcomes.

The benefits of peer practice include exposure to different personality styles and approaches, reduced coach workload allowing for more frequent practice opportunities, development of coaching skills among team members, and creation of collaborative learning cultures where team members support each other's development.

However, peer practice also presents challenges including potential for negative feedback or criticism, inconsistent quality of practice scenarios, possible reinforcement of incorrect techniques, and social dynamics that might inhibit full participation. These challenges can be managed through clear guidelines, initial coach modeling, and ongoing supervision.

Technology integration in practice sessions opens exciting possibilities while presenting some unique challenges. Video recording of practice sessions (with participant consent) can provide powerful learning tools, allowing team members to observe their own performance from an external perspective. This self-observation often leads to insights that external feedback alone cannot provide.

The measurement of role-play effectiveness requires attention to multiple dimensions including skill demonstration during practice, confidence levels before and after practice sessions, transfer of skills to real Customer interactions, and retention of skills over time. These measurements help coaches understand which practice approaches are most effective and identify team members who might need additional support.

Common practice pitfalls include attempting to practice too many skills simultaneously or in the same session, inadequate attention to emotional climate, insufficient challenge progression, poor feedback timing and quality, and failure to connect practice experiences to real-world application.

From Practice to Real-World Application

The transition from practice to real-world application represents a critical coaching moment that requires special attention and support. Team members often experience temporary performance regression as they adjust to the added complexity of real Customer interactions. This regression is normal and expected, but team members who aren't prepared for it may become discouraged and abandon newly learned techniques.

Coaches can support this transition by preparing team members for temporary difficulties, providing encouragement during challenging real-world applications, conducting brief follow-up discussions after initial real-world practice, and celebrating successful applications of practiced skills.

Advanced practice techniques can address specific learning objectives and prepare team members for complex situations they might encounter. These might include handling angry or frustrated Customers, managing multiple Customers simultaneously, dealing with technical questions beyond their expertise, or navigating price objections with budget-conscious Customers.

The customization of role-play sessions for different personality types and learning preferences requires understanding how introverts versus extroverts, detail-oriented versus big-picture learners, and competitive versus collaborative individuals respond to different practice approaches. This customization ensures that all team members can benefit from practice experiences regardless of their personal preferences or learning styles.

Cultural considerations in role-play design ensure that scenarios feel relevant and appropriate for team members from diverse backgrounds. This might involve creating Customer characters from various cultural groups, addressing different communication preferences, or adapting techniques for different cultural contexts.

The development of internal practice capabilities—teaching team members to practice with each other effectively—can significantly extend the reach and impact of coaching programs. This might involve training senior team members as practice facilitators, creating scenario libraries and practice guides, or establishing peer mentoring relationships.

Quality control in role-play sessions requires ongoing attention to scenario realism, feedback quality, emotional climate, and skill transfer outcomes. Regular evaluation of practice approaches helps ensure that sessions remain effective and valuable rather than becoming routine exercises that lose their developmental impact.

The long-term benefits of well-designed practice extend beyond specific skill development to include increased confidence in learning new skills, greater willingness to experiment with different approaches, improved ability to recover from mistakes, and enhanced overall adaptability in Customer service situations.

The masters of sales coaching understand that role-play practice is where the magic happens—where potential transforms into performance, where understanding becomes capability, and where coaching creates lasting value. When role-play sessions are designed and facilitated with skill and care, they become transformative experiences that team members value and remember long after formal coaching ends.

The ultimate goal of practice isn't perfect performance in artificial scenarios, but rather the development of confident, competent professionals who can adapt their skills to any Customer situation they encounter. When this goal is achieved, the boundary between practice and performance dissolves, creating seamless integration of skill development with daily work responsibilities.

Role-play is so significantly important to your success that we are devoting an entire chapter to it—Chapter 9. For now, let's continue our walk through the **GREAT** Sales Coaching framework.

Chapter 6

Affirm and Encourage (Keep It Positive) - The Psychology of Reinforcement

In 1965, a Harvard professor named Robert Rosenthal conducted one of the most famous experiments in educational psychology. He told elementary school teachers that certain students in their classes were "intellectual bloomers" who would show remarkable academic growth during the school year. In reality, these students were chosen completely at random. Yet by the end of the year, these randomly selected students had indeed shown significantly greater improvement than their classmates. The only difference? Their teachers' expectations and the positive attention that flowed from those expectations.

The Science of Positive Reinforcement

This "Pygmalion Effect" reveals a profound truth about human performance: what we expect from people, and how we communicate those expectations, has enormous power to shape actual outcomes. In sales coaching, this principle translates into one of the most crucial yet misunderstood aspects of development work—the strategic use of positive reinforcement to accelerate learning, build confidence, and create sustainable behavior change.

But here's where many people get confused: in the **Affirm and Encourage** *(Keep it Positive)* phase: keeping it positive doesn't mean avoiding difficult conversations, sugar-coating poor performance, or praising everything regardless of quality. True positive reinforcement is far more sophisticated than generic cheerleading—it's a precise, strategic approach to behavior modification that recognizes and rewards specific actions in ways that make those behaviors more likely to be repeated.

The science behind positive reinforcement reveals why it's so effective in learning environments. When people receive genuine, specific praise for their efforts and achievements, their brains release dopamine—a neurotransmitter that creates feelings of pleasure while simultaneously strengthening the neural pathways associated with the praised behavior. This creates what researchers call a "reinforcement loop" where positive experiences literally rewire the brain to make successful behaviors more automatic and likely.

Dr. Barbara Fredrickson's research on positive emotions at the University of North Carolina has shown that positive emotional states expand cognitive capacity, improve creative problem-solving, and increase resilience in the face of challenges. Her "broaden-and-build" theory suggests that positive emotions don't just feel good—they actually make people smarter and more capable in the moment while building psychological resources that benefit long-term performance.

This finding has profound implications for coaching effectiveness. Team members who experience consistent positive reinforcement during skill development don't just feel better about the process—they learn faster, retain more information, and transfer skills more effectively to real-world situations. And better yet, they feel better about themselves gaining much need confidence on the salesfloor.

Quality and Timing of Effective Reinforcement

However, the effectiveness of positive reinforcement depends entirely on its quality and authenticity. Research has consistently shown that generic praise ("good job," "well done," "nice work") provides minimal learning value because it doesn't specify which behaviors should be repeated. Worse, generic praise can actually undermine motivation when people perceive it as insincere or manipulative.

Effective positive reinforcement must be specific, immediate, genuine, and proportionate to the achievement. Instead of general praise, skilled coaches provide targeted feedback such as: "Your use of open-ended questions in that interaction helped you uncover the Customer's real needs, which made your product recommendation much more relevant and compelling. That's exactly the kind of consultative approach that builds Customer trust and increases sales success."

The timing of positive reinforcement significantly affects its impact on learning and behavior. Feedback provided immediately after desired behavior creates the strongest connections between actions and positive outcomes, helping team members understand exactly what they did well and increasing the likelihood they'll repeat those behaviors.

This immediacy principle explains why real-time coaching during actual Customer interactions can be so powerful, though it requires careful judgment about when and how to provide feedback without disrupting the Customer experience. Many effective coaches develop subtle signaling systems that allow them to provide immediate positive reinforcement even during live Customer interactions.

The ratio of positive to corrective feedback has been extensively studied, with fascinating results. John Gottman's research on relationship dynamics found that stable, successful relationships maintain approximately a 5:1 ratio of positive to negative interactions. Marcial Losada's research on high-performing business teams found similar ratios, with the highest-performing teams maintaining ratios between 3:1 and 6:1.

For coaching applications, this research suggests that developmental feedback should occur within a context of recognition and support. This doesn't mean avoiding necessary corrections or inflating praise but rather ensuring that team members receive abundant recognition for their efforts and progress alongside specific guidance for improvement.

Building Intrinsic Motivation and Growth Mindset

Understanding intrinsic versus extrinsic motivation becomes crucial for applying positive reinforcement effectively over time. Extrinsic motivators like bonuses, prizes, or public recognition can be effective in the short term but often lose their power over time and can sometimes actually undermine intrinsic motivation if used inappropriately.

Daniel Pink's research on motivation, popularized in his book "Drive," identifies three key elements of intrinsic motivation: autonomy (feeling of control and choice), mastery (sense of progress and improvement), and purpose (connection to meaningful goals). Effective positive reinforcement can enhance all three of these elements when applied skillfully.

For example, recognizing someone's creative problem-solving approach supports their sense of autonomy, acknowledging their skill improvement reinforces their progress toward mastery, and connecting their development to Customer service goals strengthens their sense of purpose. This multi-dimensional approach to positive reinforcement creates more sustainable motivation than simple reward systems.

The language used in positive reinforcement significantly impacts its effectiveness and long-term influence on mindset development. Carol Dweck's research on growth mindset reveals important distinctions between praise that focuses on effort and improvement versus praise that emphasizes innate ability or talent.

Saying "You worked really hard to master that technique and it shows in your improved performance" is more effective than "You're naturally good at sales" because the former reinforces the connection between effort and results while the latter suggests that ability is fixed rather than developable. Growth mindset language helps team members understand that skills can be developed through practice and persistence, which increases resilience and motivation when facing challenges.

Be Authentic

The authenticity of positive reinforcement proves crucial to its effectiveness and the coach's credibility. Team members can quickly detect insincere or manipulative praise, which can damage trust and actually decrease motivation. Effective coaches provide genuine feedback based on observed behaviors and real improvements, even if those improvements are small or incremental.

This authenticity requirement means that coaches must develop keen observation skills and learn to recognize genuine progress even in its earliest stages. Sometimes this means acknowledging effort rather than results, process improvements rather than perfect outcomes, or attitude changes rather than skill mastery.

Positive reinforcement should acknowledge not just final results but also the process and effort involved in achieving those results. Recognizing someone for their persistence in practicing new techniques, their willingness to try different approaches, or their positive attitude during challenging learning experiences reinforces the behaviors and mindsets that lead to long-term success.

This process-focused recognition is particularly important during skill development phases when results may be inconsistent or not yet optimal. Team members who receive recognition for their learning efforts are more likely to persist through the inevitable challenges that come with developing new capabilities.

The concept of "small wins," popularized by Harvard Business School professor Teresa Amabile, plays an important role in maintaining motivation during skill development. Large, complex skills can be broken down into smaller components, each of which provides opportunities for recognition and reinforcement. Acknowledging progress at each step helps maintain momentum and prevents the discouragement that can result from focusing only on final mastery.

For example, when coaching someone on Customer research or qualification techniques, small wins might include asking their first open-ended question, successfully identifying a Customer need, making an appropriate product recommendation, or handling a Customer objection professionally. Each of these components represents genuine progress worthy of recognition.

Cultural considerations significantly affect how positive reinforcement is perceived and received. Some cultures emphasize individual achievement and respond well to personal recognition, while others prioritize group harmony and prefer team-focused acknowledgment. Some cultures view direct praise as potentially embarrassing or inappropriate, while others see the absence of recognition as neglect or disrespect.

Effective coaches develop cultural intelligence around positive reinforcement, learning to adapt their recognition approaches to match individual and group preferences. This might mean providing private rather than public recognition for some team members, emphasizing team contributions rather than individual achievements, or using indirect rather than direct praise approaches.

The medium and setting for positive reinforcement can significantly impact its effectiveness and reception. While public recognition can be powerful for some team members, others prefer private acknowledgment that doesn't draw unwanted attention. Written feedback provides a permanent record that team members can refer to later, while verbal feedback allows for immediate dialogue and clarification.

The key is matching the delivery method to both the situation and the individual's preferences. This requires coaches to understand their team members well enough to know how they prefer to receive recognition and feedback.

Peer recognition can be particularly powerful in team environments where mutual support and collaboration are valued. When team members acknowledge each other's improvements and successes, it creates supportive cultures where everyone benefits from collective growth. Coaches can facilitate peer recognition by creating opportunities for team members to share successes, learn from each other, and celebrate collective achievements.

The frequency of positive reinforcement should be high during initial skill development phases and gradually decrease as behaviors become more established. This approach is actually more effective for maintaining long-term behavior than constant reinforcement.

During learning phases, frequent positive feedback helps establish new behaviors and build confidence. As skills become more automatic, intermittent reinforcement helps maintain behaviors while preventing dependence on external recognition. This progression helps team members develop internal motivation and self-reinforcement capabilities.

Creating Sustainable Positive Culture

The **Affirm and Encourage** *(Keep it Positive)* phase doesn't mean avoiding difficult conversations or failing to address performance issues. Instead, it means framing those conversations in constructive, forward-looking terms that maintain dignity and motivation while clearly identifying areas for improvement. You should always seek to speak the truth in love.

Even corrective feedback can be delivered in ways that reinforce the team member's potential and value. For example: "I know you have the capability to handle objections more effectively because I've seen you do it successfully before. Let's work on some specific techniques that can help you feel more confident when Customers express concerns."

Positive reinforcement should be connected to specific business outcomes when possible. Helping team members see the connection between their improved skills and increased sales, better Customer satisfaction, or enhanced team performance makes the reinforcement more meaningful and sustainable.

This connection might involve sharing Customer feedback about improved service, showing sales data that correlates with skill improvements, or highlighting team achievements that result from individual development efforts. When team members can see the business impact of their growth, they develop stronger motivation for continued improvement.

The long-term impact of consistent, genuine positive reinforcement extends far beyond individual skill development. Team members who receive regular recognition develop higher self-efficacy, greater resilience in facing challenges, increased willingness to take on new learning opportunities, and stronger commitment to continuous improvement.

These psychological benefits create upward spirals where confidence enables risk-taking, success builds more confidence, and learning becomes intrinsically rewarding rather than externally driven. Team members who experience this positive cycle often become advocates for coaching and development within their organizations.

Creating a culture of positive reinforcement requires consistency and commitment from all levels of leadership. When positive recognition becomes embedded in an organization's daily practices, it creates environments where excellence isn't just expected—it's naturally occurring because people feel valued, supported, and motivated to do their best work.

The measurement of positive reinforcement effectiveness can include indicators such as team member engagement levels, willingness to attempt challenging tasks, persistence in the face of difficulties, and overall job satisfaction. These metrics help coaches understand whether their recognition approaches are generating desired motivational outcomes.

Common positive reinforcement mistakes include providing praise that isn't earned or specific, over-praising to the point where recognition loses meaning, focusing only on results while ignoring effort and process, and failing to adapt recognition approaches to individual preferences and cultural backgrounds.

The mastery of positive reinforcement requires ongoing attention to authenticity, specificity, timing, and individual differences. It's both an art and a science that improves with practice, reflection, and genuine care for the people being coached.

When applied skillfully, positive reinforcement becomes a powerful catalyst for human development that goes far beyond immediate performance improvement. It creates psychological conditions where people thrive, learn continuously, and contribute their best efforts to shared goals. The investment in mastering positive reinforcement pays dividends not just in coaching effectiveness, but in the creation of work environments where everyone can flourish.

Chapter 7

Track Progress (Follow Up) - Ensuring Long-Term Success and Growth

Imagine spending months planning the perfect garden—researching the best plants, preparing the soil, purchasing quality seeds, and carefully planting everything with precision and care. Now imagine walking away and never watering, weeding, or tending to that garden again. No matter how perfect the initial preparation and planting, without ongoing care and attention, even the most promising garden will wither and die. This analogy perfectly captures why follow-up is not just important in coaching—it's absolutely essential for creating lasting change.

The last phase, **Track Progress** *(Follow Up)*, of the **GREAT** Sales Coaching framework is where coaching theory transforms into sustainable behavioral change. While the first four phases focus on immediate learning and skill development, follow-up determines whether newly learned skills become integrated into daily practice or fade away under the pressure of busy retail environments, competing priorities, and the magnetic pull of old habits.

The Science of Skill Consolidation

The neuroscience of skill development reveals why follow-up is so crucial. When people learn new skills, they initially create what researchers call "fragile neural pathways"—new connections between brain cells that enable the new behavior but aren't yet strong enough to compete effectively with established patterns. Without reinforcement and practice, these fragile pathways can quickly deteriorate, causing skills to be forgotten or abandoned within weeks of initial learning.

Remember the stats provided in Chapter 5? We lose approximately 50% of new information within the first hour after learning it! And it gets dramatically worse as the days pass.

Dr. Eric Kandel's Nobel Prize-winning research on memory and learning showed that the transformation from fragile to robust neural pathways requires what scientists call "consolidation"—the gradual strengthening of neural connections through repeated use and reinforcement. In practical (so I can understand it) terms, this means that newly learned sales techniques must be practiced regularly and supported consistently before they become natural, automatic responses that team members can rely on during high-pressure Customer interactions.

Here's where it gets really interesting: the consolidation process doesn't happen immediately or uniformly. Different aspects of new skills consolidate at different rates, and the process can be disrupted by stress, competing demands, or lack of practice opportunities. This variability explains why some team members seem to master new techniques quickly while others struggle to maintain skills they appeared to learn successfully during initial coaching sessions.

Research in organizational training effectiveness provides sobering statistics about what happens without structured follow-up. Studies consistently show that participants *retain less than 10% of newly learned skills within six months of training completion when no follow-up occurs*. Conversely, programs that include systematic follow-up activities can achieve retention rates of 85% or higher. This dramatic difference underscores why follow-up isn't optional—it's essential for achieving meaningful return on investment in coaching activities.

Structuring Effective Follow-Up Systems

The structure of effective follow-up begins during the initial coaching phases, not after they conclude. Team members should understand from the beginning that skill development is an ongoing process that extends well beyond formal role-play or training sessions. They should expect periodic check-ins, practice opportunities, and continued support as they work to integrate new skills into their daily routines.

This expectation-setting serves several important purposes: it normalizes ongoing development as a natural part of professional growth, reduces anxiety about post-coaching performance expectations, creates accountability for continued skill application, and demonstrates the organization's commitment to long-term development rather than one-time training events.

The 24-48 hour follow-up represents one of the most critical components of the entire coaching process. This initial follow-up occurs during the period when new learning is most vulnerable to decay and when team members are first attempting to apply new skills in real Customer situations. Research shows that the first few applications of newly learned skills often determine whether those skills will be integrated or abandoned.

This initial follow-up doesn't need to be lengthy or formal—it might involve a brief conversation about the team member's experience using new skills with Customers, encouragement for continued practice, and quick problem-solving around any immediate challenges encountered. The key is demonstrating ongoing support during this vulnerable transition period.

Observational follow-up involves coaches watching team members interact with real Customers to assess how well newly learned skills are being applied in actual sales situations. This type of follow-up provides the most accurate picture of skill transfer and allows coaches to identify specific areas where additional support might be needed.

However, observational follow-up must be conducted with sensitivity and skill to avoid creating performance anxiety or making Customers uncomfortable. Effective coaches position themselves where they can observe interactions without being intrusive, choose appropriate times when observation won't disrupt operations, and focus on gathering authentic performance data rather than evaluating team members during high-stress periods.

The challenge of conducting observational follow-up in busy retail environments requires creativity and flexibility. Coaches might arrange their schedules to coincide with team member shifts, use Customer service areas where observation is more natural, or create brief shadowing opportunities that feel supportive rather than evaluative.

Documentation and Follow-Up Conversations

Documentation plays a crucial role in effective follow-up by providing objective records of progress, patterns, and areas needing continued attention. Coaches should maintain records of each team member's skill development, including specific techniques practiced, performance observations, strengths demonstrated, and opportunities for continued growth.

This documentation serves multiple purposes: it provides objective data for development discussions, helps identify patterns across multiple team members, ensures continuity if coaching responsibilities change hands, and creates historical records that can inform future coaching strategies and program improvements. It also helped me when it came time for reviews. I had notes of the wok and progress the employee had made that I could reference to help in their review.

The format and tone of follow-up conversations significantly impact their effectiveness and reception. Team members need to feel that follow-up sessions are collaborative development opportunities rather than evaluative interrogations. This requires approaching follow-up conversations with genuine curiosity about their experiences, recognition of progress made, and collaborative problem-solving around any challenges encountered.

Effective follow-up conversations often begin with open-ended questions that allow team members to share their experiences in their own words. Questions like "Tell me about your experience using the new questioning techniques this week" or "What have you noticed about Customer reactions when you take time to really understand their needs?" invite reflection and self-assessment rather than defensive responses.

The frequency of follow-up activities should be customized based on individual needs, skill complexity, and progress rates. Team members who are quickly mastering new skills might need less frequent follow-up, while those facing challenges might benefit from more intensive support. This individualized approach ensures that coaching resources are allocated efficiently while meeting everyone's developmental needs.

Research on skill acquisition suggests that follow-up frequency should be highest immediately after initial learning and gradually decrease as skills become more automatic. This might mean daily check-ins during the first week, weekly conversations during the first month, and monthly follow-ups for several months thereafter, with adjustments based on individual progress and needs.

Integration with Performance Management and Technology

Group follow-up sessions can provide valuable opportunities for peer learning and mutual support when structured appropriately. When team members share their experiences applying new skills, they often learn from each other's successes and challenges while building supportive learning communities.

These sessions can help normalize the difficulties that come with changing established behaviors, provide multiple perspectives on skill application, create opportunities for peer coaching and support, and reinforce the organizational commitment to continuous development. However, group follow-up requires skilled facilitation to ensure positive, supportive atmospheres rather than comparison or complaint sessions.

The integration of follow-up activities with regular performance management processes helps ensure that coaching doesn't become an isolated activity separate from ongoing leadership responsibilities. When follow-up conversations are incorporated into regular one-on-one meetings, they become part of the natural rhythm of leadership rather than additional tasks that might be skipped when time becomes tight.

This integration also helps connect skill development with business results, career planning, and ongoing performance expectations. Team members benefit from seeing how their skill development contributes to their overall professional growth and organizational success.

Technology can enhance follow-up effectiveness when used appropriately and thoughtfully. Customer feedback systems can provide objective data about how newly learned skills are affecting Customer experiences. Sales performance dashboards can show correlations between skill application and business results. Mobile apps can provide quick check-in capabilities and progress tracking tools.

However, as I have been saying in this entire book, technology should supplement rather than replace human connection during follow-up. The relationship between coach and team member remains central to effective follow-up, and this relationship requires ongoing personal interaction, genuine conversation, and mutual respect that technology alone cannot provide.

Sustaining Long-Term Development and Results

The challenge of maintaining follow-up consistency in demanding retail environments is real and significant. Coaches often struggle to balance follow-up activities with other pressing responsibilities like inventory management, Customer service, and administrative tasks. Successful coaches address this challenge by building follow-up activities into their regular routines and viewing them as investments in long-term performance rather than additional burdens.

This perspective shift is crucial for follow-up success. When coaches view follow-up as essential business activity that generates measurable returns rather than optional extra work, they find ways to make it happen consistently even during busy periods.

Seasonal variations in retail activity can affect follow-up scheduling and approaches. During busy periods like holiday seasons, formal follow-up activities might need to be scaled back, but informal check-ins and encouragement become even more important. During slower periods, more intensive follow-up activities can help ensure continued skill development and team engagement.

The celebration of progress during follow-up activities reinforces positive behavior change and maintains motivation for continued improvement. Recognizing not just perfect performance but also effort, persistence, and incremental improvement helps team members stay engaged with the development process even when progress feels slow or difficult.

This recognition should be specific and genuine, connecting observed improvements to business outcomes when possible. For example: "I noticed how you handled that Customer's concerns about price yesterday. Your approach of acknowledging their budget constraints while highlighting the long-term value really seemed to resonate with them. That's exactly the kind of consultative selling that builds Customer trust and loyalty."

Follow-up activities should also identify when team members are ready for advanced skill development. As basic techniques become comfortable and automatic, coaches can introduce more sophisticated skills and techniques. This progressive development approach ensures that learning remains challenging and engaging while building systematically on established foundations.

The connection between the **Track Progress** *(Follow Up)* activities and sales results should be made explicit whenever possible. When team members can see how their skill development contributes to increased sales, improved Customer satisfaction, enhanced team performance, or personal career advancement, they're more likely to remain committed to continued growth and improvement.

This connection might involve sharing Customer feedback that highlights improved service, reviewing sales data that correlates with skill improvements, or discussing career advancement opportunities that become available through continued skill development.

Common follow-up pitfalls include inconsistent scheduling that sends mixed messages about priorities, focus on problems rather than progress, inadequate documentation leading to repeated discussions of the same issues, and failure to adapt follow-up approaches to individual needs and preferences.

The measurement of follow-up effectiveness can include indicators such as skill retention rates over time, successful application of techniques in Customer interactions, team member confidence and satisfaction levels, and ultimately, business results including sales performance and Customer satisfaction improvements.

Finally, follow-up activities provide valuable data for evaluating and improving coaching effectiveness overall. By tracking which techniques are most successfully implemented, which team members respond best to different coaching approaches, and which skills have the greatest impact on performance, coaches can continuously refine their methods and achieve better results with future coaching efforts.

The **Track Progress** *(Follow Up)* phase transforms coaching from a discrete training event into an ongoing development partnership. When implemented systematically and consistently, follow-up activities ensure that the time and energy invested in coaching generates lasting improvements in both individual performance and organizational capability. The coaches who master follow-up create not just temporary skill improvements, but sustainable behavior change that continues to generate value long after formal coaching relationships conclude.

The ultimate goal of effective follow-up is to help team members become self-directed learners who can continue developing their skills independently while knowing that support remains available when needed. This transformation from external dependence to internal motivation represents the highest achievement of coaching excellence.

Part 2:

Achieving Success with GREAT Sales Coaching

Chapter 8

Overcoming Resistance - Dealing with Change and Fear

Now that you know the **GREAT** Sales Coaching framework, let's do some deep dives into topics that will enhance your success level when using **GREAT** Sales Coaching with your team. Part 2 of this book focuses on the "known" issues and hurdles managers face when using **GREAT** Sales Coaching. The more you know—the better you prepare. The better you prepare—the better your sales coaching efforts.

If you've ever tried to convince a teenager to clean their room, asked your spouse to try a new restaurant, or suggested that your mother-in-law might want to consider updating her forty-year-old meatloaf recipe, you've experienced the fascinating phenomenon of psychological reactance—the almost reflexive urge to resist when we feel our freedom or autonomy is threatened. This same mechanism, which evolved to help our ancestors maintain independence in dangerous situations, kicks into high gear when adults are asked to change their professional behaviors, especially when those behaviors have served them well in the past.

Here's the delicious irony: the very people who could benefit most from coaching are often those who resist it most strongly, creating a puzzle that has challenged leadership experts for decades. It's like watching someone refuse directions while they're clearly lost, insisting they know exactly where they're going even as they drive in circles. The resistance isn't malicious or irrational—it's deeply human and surprisingly predictable once you understand the psychological forces at work.

Understanding the Psychology of Resistance

Resistance to coaching isn't a character flaw, personality defect, or sign of poor attitude—it's a completely natural human response to change that reflects deeper psychological needs for security, competence, and autonomy. Understanding this distinction is absolutely crucial because it shifts our approach from trying to "overcome" resistance through force, manipulation, or increasingly creative bribes to working with resistance as valuable information about what people need to feel safe and supported during change.

Think of resistance as the psychological equivalent of physical pain—it's an uncomfortable but useful signal that something needs attention. Just as physical pain alerts us to potential bodily harm, psychological resistance alerts us to potential threats to our identity, competence, or autonomy. The solution isn't to ignore the pain or power through it, but to understand what it's telling us and address the underlying concerns.

The roots of coaching resistance run much deeper than simple reluctance to learn new techniques or stubborn attachment to old ways of doing things. For many retail professionals, their current approach to Customer interactions represents far more than just a collection of skills—it's part of their professional identity, their source of confidence in uncertain situations, their method of maintaining control in an often-unpredictable work environment, and sometimes their only reliable source of success and recognition in their jobs.

Asking someone to change these approaches can feel like asking them to change who they are as professionals. When our sense of self feels under attack, even well-intentioned suggestions for improvement can feel like personal criticism or challenges to our competence and worth.

Dr. Robert Cialdini's research on influence and persuasion identifies several key psychological sources of resistance to change that operate largely below conscious awareness. The principle of consistency suggests that people have a powerful drive to appear consistent with their previous commitments, decisions, and beliefs. This isn't just about looking good to others—it's about maintaining a coherent sense of self in a chaotic world.

If someone has achieved success using certain sales approaches, suggesting that those approaches need improvement creates what psychologists call "cognitive dissonance"—the uncomfortable mental state that occurs when our beliefs and actions don't align. Rather than accepting that their methods might be imperfect, many people resolve this dissonance by rejecting the coaching suggestions and reinforcing their existing approaches.

The principle of autonomy, deeply rooted in self-determination theory developed by Edward Deci and Richard Ryan, suggests that people have fundamental psychological needs to feel in control of their own decisions and actions. Coaching programs that feel imposed, mandatory, or micromanaging can threaten this sense of autonomy, creating reactance even when the content is valuable and the intentions are positive.

This autonomy threat is particularly strong in sales environments where professionals often value their independence and ability to build relationships in their own style. The irony is that coaching designed to improve performance can actually harm performance if it's perceived as controlling or restrictive.

Loss aversion, first identified by behavioral economists Daniel Kahneman and Amos Tversky in their Nobel Prize-winning research, explains why people often resist change even when that change offers clear benefits. The psychological pain of giving up familiar approaches typically outweighs the potential pleasure of gaining new capabilities by a ratio of approximately 2:1. This means that for coaching to overcome natural loss aversion, the perceived benefits must be at least *twice* as compelling as the perceived costs.

This bias toward the status quo isn't laziness or stubbornness—it's an adaptive psychological mechanism that prevented our ancestors from abandoning survival strategies that were working in favor of unproven alternatives that might have gotten them killed. In modern retail environments, this same mechanism can prevent people from adopting coaching improvements that would significantly enhance their performance.

The Only Thing to Fear

Fear of incompetence represents perhaps the most significant and emotionally charged source of coaching resistance. No one wants to feel foolish or inadequate, especially in front of colleagues or Customers. Experienced sales professionals often worry that learning new techniques will temporarily reduce their effectiveness and confidence, making them feel like beginners again in areas where they previously felt competent and successful.

This fear isn't irrational—there's often a temporary performance dip when people adopt new behaviors, known in psychology as the "learning curve valley" or "conscious incompetence" phase. During this transition period, people may indeed perform worse than they did with their old methods, creating genuine risk that feeds resistance. Understanding and normalizing this temporary regression is crucial for helping people persist through the challenging adaptation period.

The phenomenon becomes even more complex when we consider that many retail professionals have been promoted or recognized based on their current approaches. Accepting coaching suggestions can feel like admitting that the very skills that brought them success are somehow inadequate—a psychologically threatening proposition that challenges not just their methods but their professional identity and self-worth.

Past negative experiences with training or coaching create another powerful source of resistance that can persist for years or even decades after the original incident. A sales professional who once endured a boring, irrelevant, or humiliating training program may approach new coaching opportunities with deep skepticism, defensive attitudes, and pre-formed expectations that must be actively addressed before meaningful learning can occur.

These past experiences create "negative transfer"—where previous learning actually interferes with new learning. The emotions and associations from past training failures can be triggered by seemingly innocuous elements of new coaching programs, such as role-playing exercises, feedback sessions, or even the simple act of being asked to learn something new.

The phenomenon of psychological reactance, first described by social psychologist Jack Brehm in the 1960s, helps explain why some people resist coaching even when they intellectually recognize its potential value. When people feel their freedom or autonomy is threatened, they experience a motivational state that drives them to restore that freedom, sometimes by rejecting helpful suggestions or resisting beneficial changes.

This reactance can be triggered by surprisingly subtle factors: language choices (being "told" what to do versus being "invited" to explore options), implementation approaches (mandatory training versus voluntary development), timing (coaching imposed during busy periods when people feel overwhelmed), or even the coach's tone of voice and body language during initial conversations.

Understanding reactance triggers allows coaches to design approaches that minimize resistance while maximizing engagement. Simple changes in presentation can dramatically affect receptivity: "You need to improve your questioning techniques" triggers reactance, while "I wonder if there are some questioning approaches that might help you feel even more confident with challenging Customers" invites collaboration.

Cultural, Generational, and Individual Differences

Cultural and generational differences add another layer of complexity to coaching resistance that requires sophisticated understanding and sensitivity. Team members from cultures that emphasize respect for experience and established hierarchies may be more resistant to suggestions for change, especially from younger coaches or those with less experience in their particular industry or role.

In some cultures, accepting coaching might be perceived as admitting weakness or incompetence, which can create shame and loss of face that generates powerful resistance. Other cultures may view coaching as disrespectful to their experience or as implying that their previous learning and development were somehow inadequate.

Generational differences can also affect coaching receptivity in ways that require thoughtful adaptation. Baby boomers who've built successful careers using certain approaches may be skeptical of new techniques promoted by younger leaders, especially if those techniques seem to contradict time-tested methods that have served them well. The resistance isn't necessarily about age or stubbornness—it often reflects legitimate concerns about abandoning proven approaches for unproven alternatives.

Generation X professionals, who came of age during corporate downsizing and economic uncertainty, may be particularly resistant to coaching that feels like preparation for replacement or evidence that their current performance is inadequate. They may interpret coaching offers as subtle criticism or signs that their job security is threatened.

Millennial and Generation Z team members, while generally more open to learning and development, may become frustrated with coaching that moves too slowly, doesn't clearly connect to career advancement, or fails to leverage technology in ways they expect. Their resistance might manifest as disengagement rather than active opposition.

Recognizing the early signs of resistance allows coaches to address concerns before they become entrenched opposition that's much more difficult to overcome. Verbal indicators include seemingly innocuous statements like "This won't work with our Customers" (translation: "I don't believe this will be effective"), "I've tried something like this before" (translation: "I've been disappointed before and don't want to be again"), "This isn't really my style" (translation: "This threatens my professional identity"), or "I don't see why we need to change what's already working" (translation: "I'm afraid of losing what makes me successful").

These statements often mask deeper concerns that need to be explored and addressed rather than simply countered with logical arguments about coaching benefits. The surface objection is rarely the real issue—it's usually a socially acceptable way of expressing deeper fears or concerns that might seem less rational or professional if stated directly.

Nonverbal resistance signs can be equally revealing and sometimes more honest than verbal responses: crossed arms or defensive body postures, minimal eye contact or distracted behavior, reluctant participation in discussions, physical withdrawal or positioning away from the coach, or facial expressions that suggest skepticism, boredom, or discomfort. While individual nonverbal behaviors can be misinterpreted, patterns of physical discomfort or disengagement often indicate underlying resistance that needs attention.

The initial response to resistance often determines whether it escalates into entrenched opposition or diminishes into collaborative problem-solving. Coaches who react defensively to resistance—becoming argumentative, insistent about the value of their methods, dismissive of concerns, or pushy about participation—typically increase resistance rather than reducing it. This defensive response triggers what psychologists call a "resistance spiral" where each party becomes more entrenched in their position and the relationship deteriorates.

It's remarkably similar to what happens in marital arguments (not that I would know): the harder one person pushes, the harder the other person pulls away, creating escalating conflict that moves further and further from productive resolution. In coaching relationships, this spiral can destroy trust and credibility that take months to rebuild.

Conversely, coaches who respond to resistance with curiosity and empathy often find that resistance diminishes as underlying concerns are addressed. This requires a fundamental shift from an advocacy mindset ("I need to convince them this is valuable") to an inquiry mindset ("I wonder what's behind their concerns and how we might address them together").

Strategies for Addressing Resistance Effectively

Active listening represents one of the most powerful tools for addressing resistance effectively, but it must be genuine listening rather than strategic waiting for your turn to talk. When team members feel truly heard and understood, their defensive mechanisms often relax, creating space for genuine dialogue about concerns and potential solutions. This means listening not just to the words being spoken, but to the emotions, fears, and underlying needs that drive those words.

For example, when a team member says, "I don't think role-playing is realistic," an effective coach might respond with something like: "It sounds like you're concerned about whether practice sessions will actually help you with real Customers. That's a completely legitimate concern. I've seen training that felt artificial and didn't translate to real situations. Can you tell me more about what feels unrealistic to you? I'd like to understand your perspective so we can find an approach that works better for you."

This response accomplishes several important things: it acknowledges the concern without being defensive, validates the legitimacy of their worry, demonstrates genuine interest in understanding their perspective, and invites collaborative problem-solving rather than adversarial debate. This approach often leads to productive conversations that reveal the real issues behind surface objections.

The technique of "finding common ground" helps reduce resistance by identifying shared goals and values that both coach and team member can support. Even resistant team members typically want to be successful in their roles, provide good Customer service, feel competent in their work, and be recognized for their contributions. By focusing on these shared objectives, coaches can frame skill development as a path toward achieving mutually desired outcomes rather than externally imposed requirements.

This might sound like: "It seems like we both want you to feel confident and successful in your Customer interactions, and we both want to make sure Customers receive the best possible service. We might have different ideas about how to achieve those goals, but we're definitely aligned on what we want to accomplish. Let's explore some options that might help you feel even more confident while still honoring your natural style and strengths."

Resistance often diminishes when people feel they have choice and control in the coaching process rather than feeling like passive recipients of predetermined training. Instead of presenting coaching as mandatory training that everyone must complete identically, effective coaches offer options and customization opportunities. This might mean allowing team members to choose which skills to focus on first, selecting their preferred practice formats, setting their own pace for skill development, or choosing when and where coaching conversations occur.

The fascinating thing about choice is that even the illusion of choice can be as powerful as actual choice in reducing reactance. Even when certain skills must be developed or certain standards must be met, coaches can offer choices about how, when, or in what sequence those requirements are addressed. This approach honors autonomy needs while still achieving coaching objectives.

The concept of "minimal viable change" can be particularly helpful when working with highly resistant team members who feel overwhelmed by the prospect of significant behavior modification. Instead of asking for dramatic changes all at once, coaches can identify the smallest possible modifications that might yield noticeable improvements. Success with small changes often builds confidence and reduces resistance to larger modifications over time.

For example, instead of asking a resistant team member to completely overhaul their greeting approach, a coach might suggest simply adding the Customer's name to their existing greeting. This minimal change is less threatening while still representing genuine improvement that can build momentum for additional development. Once the team member experiences success and positive Customer responses from this small change, they may become more open to additional modifications.

Peers Train Peers

Social proof provides another powerful tool for addressing resistance, particularly when it comes from respected peers rather than authority figures. When resistant team members see colleagues they respect successfully using new techniques and achieving better results, their resistance often begins to soften naturally. This is why having influential team members embrace coaching early in the process can have multiplying effects throughout the organization.

However, social proof must be authentic rather than manufactured or orchestrated. Resistant team members can quickly detect when peer endorsements are forced, artificial, or part of a management strategy, which can actually increase skepticism rather than reducing it. The most effective social proof comes from genuine success stories shared naturally by peers who have benefited from coaching, not from testimonials that feel scripted or mandatory.

In my workshops, I always have the peers critique and offer feedback of every roleplay scenario. Feedback coming from other members of the class is much easier to digest and feels much less threatening. It is hard not to feel "called out in front of your peers" when I give the feedback. And if you are not very careful with this, the resistance grows.

Addressing resistance requires patience and persistence without becoming pushy, manipulative, or coercive. Some team members need time to process change and come to their own conclusions about its value through observation, reflection, and gradual exposure to new ideas. Coaches who maintain supportive relationships while consistently modeling and encouraging new approaches often find that resistance diminishes naturally over extended periods.

This long-term approach requires faith in the coaching process and confidence that quality approaches will eventually speak for themselves. It also requires organizational support for coaches who are working with resistant team members, as the pressure for immediate results can tempt coaches to abandon patient approaches in favor of more coercive methods that typically backfire and create even stronger resistance.

The timing of coaching initiatives can significantly affect resistance levels across entire teams. Introducing new techniques during stressful periods like holiday seasons, major organizational changes, product launches, or personal crises often increases resistance because people are already dealing with high levels of uncertainty, pressure, and cognitive load. When possible, coaching initiatives should be timed to coincide with periods of relative stability and manageable stress levels.

However, in my experience, timing isn't always controllable. And an effective coach must learn to adapt her approach to challenging circumstances. During high-stress periods, coaches might focus more on emotional support and encouragement and less on skill development, providing stability and reassurance rather than additional challenges that might feel overwhelming.

Sometimes resistance masks deeper performance issues that need to be addressed before coaching can be effective. A team member who consistently resists skill development might be struggling with basic job requirements, facing personal challenges that affect work performance, experiencing job dissatisfaction that coaching alone cannot resolve, or dealing with interpersonal conflicts that make learning difficult.

Skilled coaches learn to recognize when resistance indicates underlying issues that require different interventions than traditional coaching. This diagnostic skill requires looking beyond surface behaviors to understand root causes of resistance and knowing when to refer team members to other resources or support systems.

The approach to resistance should be adapted to individual personalities and communication styles rather than using one-size-fits-all methods. Some people respond well to direct, logical arguments about the benefits of change supported by data and research. Others need emotional connection and relationship-based approaches that address feelings and concerns. Some prefer detailed explanations and comprehensive information, while others are more influenced by stories, examples, and peer experiences.

This customization requires coaches to develop sophisticated interpersonal skills and the ability to read individual communication preferences accurately. The same "resistance-addressing" approach that works beautifully with one person might completely fail with another, requiring coaches to maintain flexible repertoires of influence techniques.

Creating psychological safety becomes even more important when working with resistant team members who may have been criticized, dismissed, or punished for expressing concerns in the past. They need to feel that they can express concerns, ask questions, voice disagreements, and even refuse participation without facing negative consequences. This safety allows for honest dialogue about resistance sources and collaborative problem-solving around legitimate concerns.

Building psychological safety with resistant individuals often requires extra time and patience, as their resistance may stem partly from past experiences where expressing concerns led to negative consequences, ridicule, or dismissal. Coaches must demonstrate through consistent actions over time that resistance will be met with curiosity and respect rather than punishment or pressure.

Questions are the Answer

The use of questions rather than statements can be particularly effective in reducing resistance while promoting self-discovery and ownership of solutions. Instead of telling resistant team members why they should embrace new techniques, skilled coaches ask questions that help them discover potential benefits for themselves. Questions like "What would need to be true about these techniques for you to find them valuable?" or "What concerns would you need to have addressed to feel comfortable trying this approach?" invite exploration rather than triggering defensive responses.

This questioning approach requires genuine curiosity and patience, as the answers may not be what coaches expect or want to hear. However, when people feel they've reached conclusions through their own thinking rather than external pressure, they're much more likely to commit to change efforts and persist through inevitable challenges.

Follow-up becomes especially critical with resistant team members because their initial willingness to try new approaches may be fragile and easily disrupted by early setbacks, negative experiences, or return of old doubts and concerns. Frequent, supportive follow-up helps ensure that temporary difficulties don't reinforce original skepticism and cause people to abandon new techniques prematurely.

The follow-up with formerly resistant team members should be particularly sensitive to their need for autonomy and choice. Instead of checking up on compliance, effective follow-up explores their experience, addresses any challenges they're encountering, celebrates successes they're achieving, and continues to reinforce their ownership of the development process.

Building Long-Term Engagement and Transformation

The transformation of resistance into engagement often occurs gradually rather than suddenly, requiring coaches to maintain consistent support and encouragement even when progress feels painfully slow. The most resistant team members, once they become engaged, often become the most enthusiastic advocates for coaching and skill development, having overcome their initial skepticism through direct personal experience rather than external persuasion.

These transformed advocates become powerful allies in organizational culture change because their endorsement carries special credibility with other resistant team members. When someone who was initially skeptical becomes a coaching champion, it provides social proof that can be more influential than any management mandate or program promotion.

Resistance is Futile

Understanding and addressing resistance skillfully represents one of the most challenging but important aspects of coaching mastery. It requires coaches to set aside their own agenda, timeline, and ego to truly understand what people need to feel safe and supported during change. When coaches approach resistance with genuine empathy, respect, and patience, they often discover that resistance contains valuable information about how to make coaching more effective, meaningful, and sustainable.

The ultimate goal isn't to eliminate resistance entirely—some healthy skepticism and questioning improves coaching by forcing coaches to be more thoughtful, flexible, and responsive to individual needs. The goal is to transform destructive resistance that prevents learning into productive engagement that honors both individual concerns and organizational objectives. This transformation requires skill, patience, and genuine respect for the humanity and complexity of the people being coached.

When this transformation is achieved, it creates coaching relationships that are not only effective in developing skills and improving performance but also deeply satisfying and meaningful for everyone involved. The coach gains the satisfaction of helping someone overcome barriers and discover new capabilities, while the previously resistant team member experiences the pride and confidence that comes from successfully navigating change and growth. These transformed relationships often become the foundation for ongoing development partnerships that continue long after formal coaching programs end.

Chapter 9

Role-Play - Making Practice Perfect

Picture this scenario: you're learning to drive, and your instructor says, "Here's a detailed manual about operating vehicles. Study it carefully, watch some YouTube videos on how to drive, and then take the highway test next week." You'd probably think they were joking—or completely insane. Yet this is essentially how many sales training programs operate: lots of explanation, some, if any, demonstration, and then expecting people to perform flawlessly with real Customers without adequate practice opportunities.

Now, you might be reading this and thinking, didn't we already cover roleplay earlier? The answer to that question is yes and good for you noticing it - it means you are paying attention. But if there is one area of **GREAT** Sales Coaching that can have the greatest impact, it is roleplay. So, we are giving it its own chapter.

The Psychology and Science of Role-Play

Role-playing in sales coaching often evokes the same reaction as a surprise root canal appointment—groans, eyerolls, and creative excuses from team members who view it as artificial, embarrassing, or irrelevant to real Customer interactions. This resistance isn't entirely unfounded, given the unfortunate history of poorly designed role-play exercises that felt more like amateur theater productions than professional development activities.

Here's the truth - **everyone roleplays**! They either roleplay in the classroom with you or on the salesfloor with the Customer. One of those ways costs the company (and them) money and one makes them (and the company) money. But it is hard to get people to understand this truth.

When implemented with skill and sensitivity, role-play transforms from dreaded obligation into one of the most powerful tools available for developing sales expertise, building confidence, and creating breakthrough learning experiences. The key lies not in forcing reluctant participants through awkward exercises, but in revolutionizing how we think about and design practice experiences.

The resistance to role-play often stems from fundamental misunderstandings about its purpose and potential. Many people associate role-playing with childhood games, artificial training scenarios, or embarrassing team-building exercises that bear no resemblance to professional skill development. These associations create mental barriers that must be addressed before effective practice can occur.

Understanding the psychology behind effective role-play begins with recognizing that all professional interactions involve elements of performance. Sales professionals must manage their emotions, adapt their communication style, present themselves professionally, and maintain positive attitudes regardless of their internal state or personal feelings about individual Customers. Role-play simply makes this performance aspect explicit while providing safe environments to rehearse and refine these performance skills.

The concept of "deliberate practice," extensively researched by K. Anders Ericsson, provides the theoretical foundation for effective role-play design. Deliberate practice involves focused attention on specific skills, immediate feedback, and progressive challenge levels that stretch capabilities without overwhelming the performer. When role-play incorporates these elements, it becomes a powerful engine for skill development rather than an awkward exercise in pretend scenarios.

Research in cognitive psychology reveals fascinating insights about how practice affects skill development. Studies show that mental rehearsal—simply imagining oneself performing a skill—can improve actual performance almost as much as physical practice. This finding suggests that well-designed role-play scenarios can be nearly as effective as real Customer interactions for building neural pathways associated with sales skills.

The neuroscience behind this phenomenon discussed in Chapter 4, involves mirror neurons and motor cortex activation that occurs during both actual performance and vivid imagination of performance. When people engage in realistic role-play scenarios, their brains literally rehearse the skills being practiced, creating stronger neural connections that improve real-world performance.

Creating Safe Practice Environments

Creating psychological safety represents perhaps the most critical element of successful role-play programs. Team members must feel safe to make mistakes, try new approaches, and receive feedback without fear of judgment, ridicule, or negative consequences. This safety is established through coach behavior, environmental design, ground rules, and overall organizational culture surrounding skill development activities.

Psychological safety in role-play environments requires explicit attention to power dynamics, social relationships, and individual comfort levels. Some team members may feel vulnerable practicing in front of colleagues, while others worry about appearing incompetent in front of supervisors. These concerns must be acknowledged and addressed directly rather than dismissed or ignored. But this does not mean you do not roleplay in front of others. It simply means that there is some preparation work you need to do before you begin.

Set the Ground Rules

The physical environment for role-play matters more than many coaches realize. Private spaces where participants don't worry about being observed or overheard create better learning conditions than public areas where self-consciousness might interfere with practice. Comfortable seating, appropriate lighting, freedom from interruptions, and informal atmospheres all contribute to environments where participants can focus on learning rather than managing anxiety about the setting.

Ground rules for role-play sessions should be established clearly and reinforced consistently. These might include agreements about confidentiality (what happens in practice stays in practice), respect (feedback focuses on behaviors rather than personalities), support (everyone is here to help each other improve), and growth mindset (mistakes are learning opportunities rather than failures).

When participants understand and agree to these parameters, they can engage more fully in the learning process without expending mental energy on social concerns or self-protection behaviors that interfere with skill development.

Designing Effective Scenarios and Customer Characters

The structure of individual role-play scenarios significantly affects their learning value and participant engagement. Scenarios should be realistic enough to feel relevant and meaningful but controlled enough to allow for focused skill practice. This often means starting with relatively straightforward Customer situations and gradually introducing complexity as participants become more comfortable and skilled.

Scenario design should consider specific learning objectives for each practice session. A role-play focused on greeting techniques might feature a friendly, responsive Customer who provides positive feedback to various approaches, allowing participants to experiment with different greeting styles and observe their effects. Conversely, a session focused on handling objections might feature a Customer who raises specific concerns that require particular response techniques.

The key is to prepare the "Customer" in your roleplay as well as the sales professional. Make sure the Customer is realistic. Retailers in a roleplay scenario often want to be the difficult or problem Customer that they actually experience in the store before.

Play the Percentages

The progression of scenario difficulty should follow principles of optimal challenge—providing enough stretch to promote growth without creating overwhelming stress that impairs learning. Early scenarios might involve very cooperative Customers who respond positively to all techniques, while advanced scenarios might include time pressure, multiple Customers, or complex product comparisons.

The coach's role during role-play scenarios is multifaceted and demanding, requiring simultaneous attention to multiple elements: providing realistic Customer responses, observing participant behavior, monitoring emotional states, identifying teachable moments, and maintaining scenario flow. This complexity explains why effective role-play coaching typically occurs one-on-one rather than in large groups where attention becomes too divided.

Customer character development represents an often-overlooked aspect of effective role-play that can dramatically impact learning outcomes. Coaches who play Customers should create consistent, believable characters with specific backgrounds, needs, communication styles, and decision-making patterns. These characters should be challenging enough to provide realistic practice opportunities but not so difficult that they discourage participants or prevent skill application.

The development of multiple Customer personas allows participants to practice adapting their approaches to various personality types and situations. A rushed business Customer requires different techniques than a leisurely browser, and a technically knowledgeable Customer needs different treatment than someone who's new to the product category. Practicing with diverse Customer types builds adaptability and confidence.

But, as I said earlier, play the percentages. It's true that a Customer might ask for something "off the wall", but make sure your roleplay scenarios are in the 80% of what actually happens and stay out of the 20% of what sometimes happens.

Clear, Concise Feedback

Feedback delivery during and after role-play scenarios requires careful attention to timing, content, and emotional tone. Interrupting scenarios to provide immediate feedback can disrupt learning flow and break participants' engagement with the practice situation. However, waiting until scenarios conclude might mean missing important teachable moments or allowing incorrect techniques to be repeated without correction.

The most effective approach often involves allowing scenarios to reach natural conclusion points before providing comprehensive feedback, while making brief, supportive comments during natural breaks in the interaction. This balance maintains scenario flow while ensuring that important learning opportunities aren't missed.

The structure of feedback conversations significantly affects their impact on learning and participant motivation. Effective feedback typically begins with participant self-assessment ("What do you think went well in that interaction?"), followed by specific positive observations, then targeted suggestions for improvement, and finally collaborative planning for the next practice attempt.

This structure promotes reflection and self-awareness while maintaining motivation through recognition of strengths and progress. When feedback feels like collaborative exploration rather than critical evaluation, participants remain open to learning and willing to take risks during subsequent practice attempts.

Video recording of role-play sessions, when used with full participant consent and appropriate sensitivity, can dramatically enhance learning effectiveness. Watching their own performance allows participants to observe behaviors they might not have been aware of during the interaction, leading to insights that external feedback alone cannot provide. And since everyone has a smartphone these days, recording is very easy to do. You do not need anything more elaborate than the device we all talk on all day long.

The power of video feedback lies in its objectivity and specificity. Instead of relying on verbal descriptions of behaviors, participants can see exactly what they did and how it appeared to others. This visual feedback often leads to "aha moments" where participants suddenly understand how their actions affect Customer perceptions and responses.

However, video recording should be introduced gradually and used sensitively, as some participants may initially feel self-conscious about being recorded. The technology should enhance rather than complicate the learning process, and recorded sessions should be used solely for developmental purposes with strict agreements about confidentiality and storage.

I cannot tell you how many times someone is doing well with their role-plays and learning—until that red light on the camera turns on. It makes us self-conscience. So keep that in mind when you are recording. Give them a chance to get comfortable with the process reminding them that the video is for them and not for anyone else.

Break it Down

Progressive skill building through role-play requires careful attention to sequencing and pacing that respects natural learning processes. Rather than attempting to practice entire sales processes in single sessions, effective coaches break complex skills into manageable components that can be mastered individually before being combined into more sophisticated performances.

This approach prevents mental overload while building confidence systematically through incremental success experiences. For example, greeting techniques might be practiced and mastered before moving to questioning strategies, which are developed before practicing product recommendations or demonstrations, and so forth through the entire sales process.

The concept of "errorless learning" suggests that practice sessions should be structured to maximize success experiences while still providing appropriate challenges. This doesn't mean making role-plays unrealistically easy, but rather designing scenarios that allow participants to experience success while stretching their capabilities in manageable increments.

Success breeds confidence, and confidence enables risk-taking and experimentation—both essential elements of effective skill development. Participants who experience early success in role-play are more likely to persist through challenges, try new approaches, and transfer skills to real Customer interactions.

Peer-to-peer role-play can add valuable dimensions to skill development when managed appropriately and sensitively. Team members practicing with each other can provide different perspectives, share varied approaches, create supportive learning communities, and reduce dependency on coach availability for practice opportunities.

The benefits of peer practice include exposure to different personality styles and approaches, increased practice frequency through reduced coach workload, development of coaching and feedback skills among team members, and creation of collaborative learning cultures where mutual support is valued and expected.

However, peer role-play also presents challenges that must be carefully managed: potential for negative feedback or unconstructive criticism, inconsistent quality of practice scenarios, possible reinforcement of incorrect techniques, and social dynamics that might inhibit full participation or create competitive rather than supportive atmospheres. (Keep in mind that by peer role-play I am referring to your learner practicing with his or her peers without you present.)

These challenges can be addressed through clear guidelines and expectations, initial coach modeling of effective feedback approaches, ongoing supervision and quality control, and careful attention to group composition and dynamics.

Advanced Techniques and Cultural Impact

Advanced role-play techniques can address specific learning objectives and challenge experienced participants who have mastered basic skills. These might include handling angry or frustrated Customers, managing multiple Customers simultaneously, dealing with technical questions beyond one's expertise, navigating price objections with budget-conscious Customers, or managing time effectively during busy periods.

Advanced scenarios should be introduced only after participants have developed confidence and competence with fundamental skills. The progression from basic to advanced practice should mirror the natural development of expertise, building systematically on established foundations rather than jumping prematurely to complex challenges.

The integration of role-play with real-world application represents a crucial transition that requires special attention and support. Participants need to understand how practice scenarios relate to actual Customer situations they'll encounter, and they should be encouraged to apply newly practiced techniques in real interactions as soon as possible after role-play sessions.

This transfer process can be supported through debriefing discussions that explicitly connect practice experiences to real-world applications, follow-up conversations that explore initial attempts to use new skills with Customers, and ongoing coaching that helps participants adapt techniques to their unique Customer base and work environment.

The measurement of role-play effectiveness requires attention to both immediate learning outcomes and longer-term skill transfer results. Immediate indicators might include participant engagement levels, skill demonstration during practice sessions, confidence improvements, and feedback quality. Longer-term measures could include skill application in real Customer interactions, performance improvements, and retention of practiced techniques over time.

These measurements help coaches understand which role-play approaches are most effective for different types of learners and learning objectives, enabling continuous improvement of practice design and facilitation methods.

The cultural impact of successful role-play programs extends beyond individual skill development to influence overall team dynamics and organizational learning culture. When role-play becomes normalized and valued rather than dreaded and avoided, it creates environments where continuous learning is expected, mistakes are viewed as learning opportunities, and skill development becomes a shared responsibility among team members.

This cultural transformation often begins with individual positive experiences that change attitudes about practice and learning. As more team members experience the benefits of effective role-play, enthusiasm spreads naturally throughout the organization, creating momentum for expanded coaching and development activities.

Use Triads

One of the best tools I use in my workshops when it comes to role-play is the use of triads. When you are in a group setting, the best role-play sessions allow for practice at the tables before they get in front of the room. Put the team members into groups of three. (If you have one left over, its okay to have four in a group.)

Assign each of the three a role for the role-play - Sales Professional, Customer, Observer. Then have them complete the role-play practice. The role of the Observer is just as it sounds—they observe the role-play and then when done, provide feedback to the Sales Professional on what he did well and what he might try next time to improve.

First, this puts you in the "peers training peers" mode which we have stated is often more effective for learning. Second, hearing feedback from the "independent" Observer versus the person leading the workshop or practice session is way more likely to be accepted and heard. Then, when it is their turn to role-play in front of the room, this triad experience will have helped them "tweak" their role-play performance allowing them to look better in front of a room full of their peers.

Rotate the scenario three times allowing each person in the triad to serve each role. So now the Sales Professional becomes the Customer and the Observer becomes the Sales Professional and so on. If you do have a group with four, then have two Observers each round.

The Future is Now

The future of role-play in sales coaching will likely incorporate advancing technologies while maintaining focus on human connection and relationship building. Virtual reality systems may provide more immersive practice environments, artificial intelligence might enable more sophisticated Customer simulations, and mobile technologies could make practice opportunities more accessible and convenient.

However, the fundamental principles of effective role-play—psychological safety, progressive challenge, realistic scenarios, quality feedback, and skill transfer support—will remain constant regardless of technological advances. The most effective future approaches will blend technological capabilities with human insight, using tools to enhance rather than replace the interpersonal elements that make coaching transformational.

The mastery of role-play facilitation represents a crucial competency for sales coaches that requires ongoing development and refinement. Like other coaching skills, role-play facilitation improves through deliberate practice, feedback, and continuous learning. Coaches who commit to mastering this art create learning experiences that are both memorable and transformational, turning the dreaded "R-word" into a powerful catalyst for professional growth and development.

Chapter 10

Building a Culture of Continuous Improvement - Intrinsic Motivation

Imagine walking into a retail store where every team member is genuinely excited about getting better at their job, where colleagues spontaneously share techniques that work well with Customers, where mistakes are treated as learning laboratories rather than failures, and where the question "How can we do this better?" is asked naturally and regularly rather than forced through management mandates. This isn't a fantasy—it's what happens when organizations successfully create cultures of continuous improvement. But here's the challenge: culture can't be mandated, purchased, or installed like new software. It must be carefully cultivated, consistently nurtured, and patiently grown over time.

Understanding Organizational Culture and Its Components

Creating a culture where continuous improvement thrives requires far more than implementing coaching programs or conducting training sessions. It demands a fundamental transformation in how an organization thinks about learning, growth, excellence, and the very nature of work itself. This cultural transformation doesn't happen through policy changes or mission statement revisions—it emerges through consistent leadership behaviors, systematic support for development activities, and the gradual establishment of norms and expectations that make continuous learning feel natural rather than exceptional.

The concept of organizational culture, while sometimes dismissed as touchy-feely management speak, has concrete, measurable impacts on employee behavior, Customer satisfaction, and business results. Culture consists of the shared beliefs, values, and assumptions that guide how people behave when no one is watching—or perhaps more accurately, when everyone is watching but no one is explicitly directing.

Edgar Schein, the MIT professor who pioneered organizational culture research, identified three levels of culture: artifacts (visible behaviors and symbols), espoused values (stated beliefs and principles), and basic assumptions (unconscious beliefs that actually drive behavior). Most culture change efforts focus only on the first two levels while ignoring the deep assumptions that determine how people act. Effective continuous improvement cultures must address all three levels systematically and consistently.

In my book, **Culturrific!**, I break corporate culture into five elements: Behaviors, Folklore, Communication, Values and Beliefs. And, honestly, I would rather refer you to that book for more detail than to get too far off track in this book - if you know what I mean.

Building Psychological Safety and Growth Mindset

Research in organizational psychology has identified several key characteristics that distinguish high-learning cultures from those where development remains sporadic or superficial. These include psychological safety (people feel safe to admit mistakes and ask questions), growth mindset (abilities are viewed as developable rather than fixed), learning orientation (emphasis on development alongside performance), collaboration (knowledge sharing is valued and rewarded), and leadership modeling (leaders actively demonstrate learning behaviors).

Psychological safety, as defined by Harvard Business School professor Amy Edmondson, represents the foundation upon which all other cultural elements rest. When team members fear negative consequences for admitting knowledge gaps, making mistakes, or asking for help, they naturally become defensive and resistant to learning opportunities. This fear creates what researchers call "defensive routines"—behaviors designed to protect self-image and avoid embarrassment rather than promote growth and improvement.

Conversely, when people feel safe to be vulnerable and take learning risks, they become more engaged in development activities, more likely to transfer new skills to their work, more willing to seek feedback and help, and more inclined to share their own knowledge and insights with others. Psychological safety doesn't mean lowering performance standards or avoiding difficult conversations—it means creating environments where people can focus on getting better rather than looking good.

Creating psychological safety begins with leadership behavior and gradually permeates throughout the organization as team members observe and internalize new norms. Leaders who admit their own learning needs, share stories about mistakes they've made and lessons learned, ask genuine questions about how to improve, and respond supportively to team member questions and errors help establish environments where learning becomes safe and expected rather than risky and exceptional.

The growth mindset concept, popularized by Stanford psychologist Carol Dweck, distinguishes between organizations that view abilities as fixed traits and those that see them as qualities that can be developed through effort, strategy, and support. In fixed mindset cultures, people tend to avoid challenges that might reveal limitations, hide mistakes to preserve their image of competence, resist feedback that suggests areas for improvement, and view others' success as threatening to their own status.

Growth mindset cultures, conversely, encourage challenge-seeking, view mistakes as learning opportunities, embrace feedback as valuable information for development, and celebrate others' success as proof that improvement is possible. The language used throughout the organization reflects these different mindsets: fixed mindset cultures emphasize natural talent and innate ability, while growth mindset cultures focus on effort, strategy, and improvement.

Transforming from fixed to growth mindset requires careful attention to recognition systems, problem-solving approaches, and communication patterns throughout the organization. Instead of praising natural talent ("You're a born salesperson"), growth-oriented cultures recognize effort and strategy ("Your preparation and questioning technique really paid off with that Customer"). Instead of hiding failures or assigning blame when things go wrong, they conduct learning-focused post-mortems that identify system improvements and skill development opportunities.

It's About Learning Not Performing

Learning orientation versus performance orientation represents another crucial cultural dimension that affects how people approach their work and development. Performance-oriented cultures focus primarily on results and outcomes, sometimes at the expense of the learning and development that enable sustainable high performance. This can create environments where people become risk-averse, hide problems until they become critical, and prioritize short-term results over long-term capability building.

Learning-oriented cultures balance attention to results with investment in the capabilities that drive those results. They understand that sustainable high performance requires continuous capability development, that temporary performance dips during learning are normal and acceptable, and that investing in people's growth ultimately generates superior business results. This doesn't mean caring less about performance—learning-oriented cultures often achieve superior long-term results because they build the capabilities necessary for sustained excellence.

Collaboration and knowledge sharing distinguish high-learning cultures from those where information hoarding and territorial behavior limit organizational capability development. In collaborative cultures, sharing knowledge and helping others develop is viewed as valuable behavior that enhances both individual and organizational success. Team members who discover effective techniques or solve challenging problems are expected and encouraged to share their insights with colleagues.

Creating collaborative learning cultures requires intentional system design and consistent reinforcement. This might involve establishing regular knowledge-sharing meetings where team members present successful techniques or interesting challenges, creating mentoring programs that pair experienced performers with newcomers, developing recognition systems that reward helping others succeed, or designing work processes that require collaboration and mutual support.

The key is making collaboration and knowledge sharing easier and more rewarding than information hoarding or working in isolation. This often requires addressing competitive elements in performance management systems that might inadvertently discourage collaboration, creating time and space for knowledge sharing activities, and recognizing collaborative behaviors alongside individual achievements.

Be the Change

Leadership modeling plays a crucial role in cultural transformation because team members pay far more attention to what leaders do than what they say. Leaders who consistently demonstrate learning behaviors—asking questions, seeking feedback, admitting when they don't know something, and investing visible time in their own development—send powerful messages about organizational values and expectations.

However, leadership modeling must be authentic rather than performative to have lasting cultural impact. Team members can quickly detect when leaders are going through the motions of learning behaviors without genuine commitment to growth and development. Authentic modeling requires leaders to engage in learning activities, struggle with new skills, demonstrate the vulnerability that comes with genuine development efforts, and show real commitment to their own continuous improvement.

The role of systems and processes in supporting continuous improvement culture cannot be overlooked. Cultures are sustained by the formal and informal systems that reinforce desired behaviors and discourage counterproductive ones. This includes hiring processes that prioritize learning orientation and growth mindset, performance management systems that balance results with development, promotion criteria that value coaching and mentoring capabilities, and resource allocation decisions that demonstrate genuine commitment to learning and development.

When organizational systems are aligned with stated cultural values, they reinforce and strengthen cultural transformation efforts. When systems contradict stated values—for example, promoting only top performers regardless of their development of others, or cutting training budgets when financial pressure increases—they undermine culture change efforts and create cynicism about leadership commitment.

Honestly, when we were all dealing with the COVID pandemic, training budgets were the first to be cut. But the truth was, we had more time than ever to invest in our people since the level of business was down for that season.

Communication, Measurement, and Resistance Management

Communication strategies play a vital role in cultural transformation by helping team members understand the rationale behind continuous improvement initiatives, their role in making them successful, and the benefits they can expect from active participation. Effective communication goes beyond announcing new programs or policies to include storytelling that illustrates the value of learning, recognition of improvement efforts and achievements, and ongoing dialogue about challenges and successes in skill development.

The most powerful communication often comes through stories rather than policies or presentations. When leaders share specific examples of how learning and development have contributed to individual and organizational success, these stories create emotional connection and practical understanding that formal communications cannot achieve. Stories make abstract concepts concrete and help people visualize how continuous improvement might benefit them personally.

The measurement of cultural change requires attention to both leading indicators (behaviors that predict cultural shifts) and lagging indicators (outcomes that result from cultural changes). Leading indicators might include participation rates in development activities, frequency of peer-to-peer coaching interactions, number of improvement suggestions submitted by team members, or employee engagement survey responses related to learning and development.

Lagging indicators could include employee retention rates, Customer satisfaction improvements, sales performance increases, or innovation metrics that suggest organizational adaptability and growth. The key is establishing measurement systems that capture both the behaviors that drive cultural change and the outcomes that result from successful cultural transformation.

Resistance to cultural change is natural and should be expected and planned for rather than viewed as a sign of program failure. Some team members may resist continuous improvement initiatives because they challenge established ways of working, require new skills and behaviors, create uncertainty about future expectations, or threaten existing power structures and status hierarchies.

Addressing cultural resistance requires many of the same approaches used for individual coaching resistance: understanding underlying concerns, providing clear benefits and rationale, offering choices and involvement in implementation, demonstrating consistent leadership commitment, and maintaining patience during the extended time periods that cultural change typically requires.

The pace of cultural transformation varies significantly across organizations and depends on factors such as current culture strength, leadership commitment and consistency, resource availability, external pressures, and organizational size and complexity. Some organizations may see significant cultural shifts within months, while others require years of consistent effort to achieve lasting transformation.

Understanding and communicating realistic timelines helps maintain commitment and momentum during periods when progress may feel slow or invisible. Cultural change often happens gradually and then suddenly, with long periods of seemingly minimal progress followed by rapid shifts as new norms reach critical mass and become self-reinforcing.

How Much Do You Value Training?

Sustainability of continuous improvement culture requires embedding learning and development into the fabric of daily operations rather than treating them as separate activities that occur during designated training times or special events. This integration might involve incorporating skill practice into regular team meetings, making coaching conversations part of routine performance discussions, creating opportunities for on-the-job learning and experimentation, or establishing peer learning partnerships that operate continuously rather than episodically.

The business case for continuous improvement culture becomes stronger over time as organizations experience benefits such as improved employee engagement and retention, enhanced Customer experience and loyalty, increased innovation and adaptability, superior financial performance, and enhanced reputation as an employer of choice. These benefits often take time to materialize fully, but they provide compelling justification for continued investment in cultural transformation efforts.

Cross-functional collaboration in continuous improvement initiatives helps ensure that learning and development become organizational priorities rather than departmental concerns. When sales, operations, human resources, and leadership teams work together to support continuous improvement culture, it sends clear messages about organizational commitment while creating more comprehensive support systems for learning activities.

The evolution of continuous improvement culture often progresses through predictable stages that organizations can recognize and plan for: initial awareness and interest in learning and development concepts, experimentation with new approaches and programs, integration of successful practices into regular operations, normalization of learning behaviors as standard expectations, and finally, innovation and continuous refinement of improvement processes.

Understanding these developmental stages helps leaders provide appropriate support and maintain realistic expectations throughout the transformation process. Different stages require different types of leadership attention, resource allocation, and communication strategies to maintain momentum and progress toward cultural goals.

External partnerships can accelerate cultural transformation by providing expertise, resources, and outside perspectives that internal teams might lack. These partnerships might involve training organizations with specialized expertise in culture change, industry associations that provide benchmarking and best practice sharing, educational institutions that offer research-based insights, or peer companies that have successfully implemented continuous improvement cultures.

However, external partnerships should supplement rather than replace internal leadership commitment and capability development. Culture change ultimately **must** be owned and driven by internal leaders who understand the organization's unique context, challenges, and opportunities. External partners can provide valuable support and expertise, but they cannot create lasting culture change without deep internal commitment and consistent effort.

The legacy of successful continuous improvement culture transformation extends far beyond individual organizations to influence industry standards, Customer expectations, and community development. Organizations that successfully create cultures of continuous learning often become employers of choice in their markets, industry leaders in Customer experience---The legacy of successful continuous improvement culture transformation extends far beyond individual organizations to influence industry standards, Customer expectations, and community development. Organizations that successfully create cultures of continuous learning often become employers of choice in their markets, industry leaders in Customer service and innovation, and positive influences on their broader business communities.

These organizations develop reputations that attract top talent, create Customer experiences that set new standards for their industries, and contribute to raising the overall quality of business practices in their communities. The ripple effects of culture transformation can influence suppliers, competitors, and even Customers who experience what's possible when organizations truly commit to continuous improvement.

The technology revolution presents both opportunities and challenges for building continuous improvement cultures. Digital platforms can facilitate knowledge sharing, provide access to learning resources, enable peer-to-peer coaching across geographic boundaries, and create data-driven insights about learning and development effectiveness. Mobile technologies can make learning opportunities more accessible and convenient, while social platforms can build learning communities that extend beyond traditional organizational boundaries.

However, technology can also create temptations to substitute digital solutions for human connection and relationship building that remain central to effective culture change. The most successful approaches blend technological capabilities with interpersonal development, using tools to enhance rather than replace the human elements that make cultures truly transformational.

The measurement and monitoring of culture change requires sophisticated approaches that capture both quantitative indicators and qualitative shifts in organizational life. Traditional employee surveys can provide valuable baseline and progress data, but they must be supplemented with observational methods, focus groups, story collection, and other techniques that capture the nuanced ways culture manifests in daily work experiences.

Culture measurement should also account for subcultures within larger organizations, as different departments, locations, or teams may experience culture change at different rates and in different ways. Understanding these variations helps leaders provide targeted support where needed while celebrating progress where it's occurring naturally.

It Must Be Part of the Fabric of Your Business Strategy

The integration of continuous improvement culture with business strategy ensures that learning and development efforts remain aligned with organizational goals and market realities. Culture change initiatives that operate independently of business strategy often lose momentum and support over time, while those that clearly contribute to strategic objectives gain strength and sustainability.

This integration requires ongoing dialogue between leadership teams about how culture supports business objectives, regular assessment of whether culture initiatives are contributing to desired business outcomes, and adjustment of culture change efforts based on evolving business needs and market conditions.

The development of internal culture change capabilities ensures that transformation efforts can be sustained and evolved over time without constant dependence on external support. This might involve training internal change agents who can facilitate culture development activities, creating systems for identifying and developing cultural ambassadors throughout the organization, or establishing ongoing processes for monitoring and adjusting culture change efforts.

Building internal capability also includes developing leaders at all levels who understand culture change principles and can support transformation efforts through their daily actions and decisions. When culture change becomes part of every leader's responsibility rather than a specialized function, it becomes more sustainable and comprehensive.

The celebration and recognition of culture change milestones helps maintain momentum and engagement throughout extended transformation processes. Culture change can feel abstract and slow-moving, making it important to identify and celebrate concrete indicators of progress along the way.

These celebrations might recognize individuals who exemplify desired cultural behaviors, teams that achieve learning and development milestones, or organizational achievements that result from improved culture. The key is making culture change feel real and meaningful rather than theoretical or distant.

Quality assurance in culture change efforts requires ongoing attention to whether initiatives are producing desired outcomes, whether implementation remains true to stated values and principles, and whether culture change efforts are having unintended consequences that need to be addressed.

This might involve regular check-ins with employees about their experience of culture change, monitoring of key culture indicators over time, and willingness to adjust approaches when data suggests they're not producing desired results. Culture change is too important and too complex to implement without careful attention to effectiveness and course correction when needed.

The global and diverse nature of modern workforces adds complexity to culture change efforts that must be acknowledged and addressed thoughtfully. Different cultural backgrounds, generational perspectives, and life experiences can influence how people respond to culture change initiatives, requiring approaches that honor diversity while building unity around shared values and goals.

This cultural competence requires leaders who understand how their own cultural backgrounds influence their perspectives, sensitivity to how culture change initiatives might be perceived by people from different backgrounds, and ability to adapt approaches while maintaining core principles and objectives.

The future evolution of continuous improvement cultures will likely incorporate insights from positive psychology, neuroscience research, and organizational behavior studies that continue to deepen our understanding of what makes cultures effective and sustainable. However, the fundamental principles of culture change—leadership modeling, system alignment, consistent communication, patient persistence, and genuine care for people's development—will likely remain constant.

The organizations that master culture change will continue to have significant competitive advantages in attracting talent, serving Customers, and adapting to changing market conditions. These advantages will become even more important as business environments become more complex and change occurs at ever-increasing rates.

The creation of continuous improvement cultures represents one of the most challenging and rewarding aspects of organizational leadership. It requires vision, patience, consistency, and genuine belief in people's potential for growth and development. When successful, it creates workplaces where people thrive, Customers receive exceptional service, and organizations achieve sustainable success that benefits all stakeholders.

The investment in culture change pays dividends that extend far beyond immediate business results to encompass human development, community contribution, and the creation of organizational legacies that influence people's careers and lives long after they move on to other opportunities. For leaders willing to make this investment, the rewards are both personally and professionally transformational.

I know this may sound self-serving, but I do recommend you checking out the book **Culturrific!** to get a deep dive into culture change and Customer experience. This chapter was meant to demonstrate how important culture change is in your organization to see real, lasting change in behavior from your **GREAT** Sales Coaching.

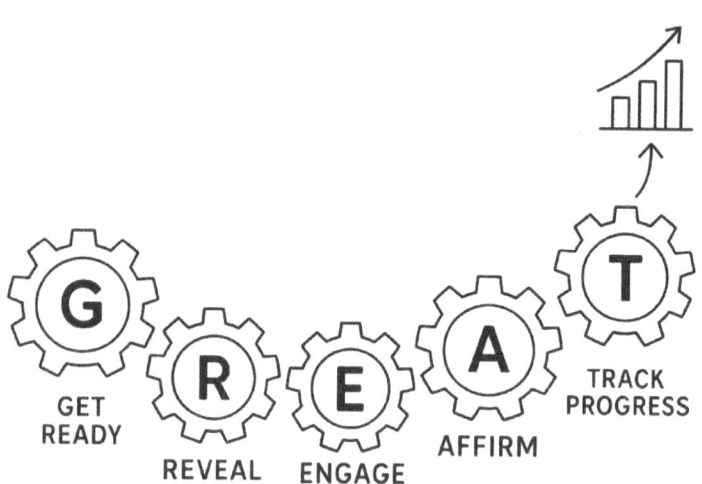

Chapter 11

Advanced Coaching Techniques - Adapting to Different Learning Styles

Walk into any bookstore and you'll find dozens of books claiming that people are either "visual," "auditory," or "kinesthetic" learners, as if human beings were simple machines that could be programmed with a single input method. The reality of how people learn is far more fascinating and complex than these oversimplified categories suggest. While individuals do have learning preferences and strengths, the most effective coaching approaches recognize that optimal learning occurs when multiple pathways are engaged simultaneously, creating rich, multi-dimensional experiences that honor individual differences while maximizing learning effectiveness for everyone.

Understanding Learning Complexity Beyond Simple Categories

The recognition that people learn differently isn't a new concept. Educators have observed learning variations for centuries. However, the application of this knowledge to sales coaching requires sophisticated understanding that goes far beyond matching training methods to supposed learning "types." Advanced coaching moves from one-size-fits-all approaches to embrace personalized development strategies that consider not just learning preferences, but also cognitive processing styles, personality differences, cultural backgrounds, motivational drivers, and individual life experiences that shape how people approach new learning.

The foundation of learning style theory rests on the understanding that while all humans share basic learning mechanisms—we all have brains that process information, form memories, and develop skills—there are significant individual variations in how people prefer to receive, process, and apply new information. These preferences aren't just random quirks; they often reflect deeper patterns of cognitive processing that have developed over years of education and experience.

However, modern neuroscience research has revealed that learning styles are more nuanced and flexible than early theories suggested. Rather than having single, fixed learning preferences that never change, most people employ multiple learning modalities simultaneously and can develop their capacity to learn through less preferred channels. This understanding has led to more sophisticated coaching approaches that leverage multiple learning channels while still acknowledging individual preferences and strengths.

Dr. Howard Gardner's theory of multiple intelligences expanded our understanding of learning differences by identifying eight distinct types of intelligence: linguistic, logical-mathematical, spatial, bodily-kinesthetic, musical, interpersonal, intrapersonal, and naturalist. You might recognize yourself in more than one of those eight. This framework suggests that people may have different strengths across various domains, and that effective coaching should engage multiple types of intelligence rather than focusing solely on traditional verbal-linguistic approaches.

The Visual

Visual learners in sales coaching environments often benefit from techniques that make abstract concepts concrete and visible. This might involve creating flowcharts that map sales processes, using diagrams to illustrate Customer journey stages, developing visual aids that highlight key conversation techniques, or employing color-coding systems that help organize information logically.

For visual learners, role-play sessions might include written cue cards that remind them of key techniques, process maps that they can reference during practice, or even video recordings that allow them to observe their own performance from an external perspective. The challenge with visual learners often lies in helping them translate visual understanding into fluid verbal performance during Customer interactions.

Coaches working with visual learners might use techniques such as mind mapping to help organize thoughts before role-play sessions, creating visual reminders that can be referenced during practice, using gestures and body language that reinforce verbal techniques, or developing visual metaphors that make abstract concepts more concrete and memorable.

The Auditory

Auditory learners typically respond well to coaching approaches that emphasize discussion, verbal feedback, and hearing techniques explained from multiple perspectives. These learners often benefit from coaching conversations that include extensive dialogue about techniques, Customer psychology, and the reasoning behind specific approaches. They may also respond well to listening to recordings of excellent Customer interactions or participating in group discussions where they can hear different viewpoints about sales strategies.

For auditory learners, the coach's tone of voice, pace of speech, and verbal emphasis become particularly important elements of effective coaching. These learners are often more sensitive to the emotional undertones of feedback and may require more verbal encouragement and support than their visual or kinesthetic counterparts. They also tend to benefit from verbal rehearsal of key phrases and techniques before attempting role-play scenarios.

Coaches can enhance learning for auditory processors by encouraging them to "think out loud" during problem-solving, providing rich verbal explanations of techniques and strategies, using varied vocal tones and pacing to maintain engagement, and creating opportunities for verbal processing of experiences and insights.

The Kinesthetic

Kinesthetic learners need hands-on experience and physical practice to develop sales skills effectively. These learners often struggle with traditional classroom-style training but excel when given opportunities to practice techniques immediately and repeatedly. Coaching approaches for kinesthetic learners should emphasize frequent role-play sessions, real-world application opportunities, and physical elements that reinforce learning.

The challenge with kinesthetic learners often lies in providing enough practice opportunities within the constraints of busy retail environments. Creative coaches might establish brief, frequent practice sessions throughout the workday, create opportunities for shadowing experienced team members while selling, or develop practice scenarios that can be conducted during quiet periods on the sales floor.

Kinesthetic learners benefit from coaching approaches that incorporate movement and physical activity, use props and manipulatives during training, provide frequent breaks for physical activity, and connect abstract concepts to concrete, tactile experiences.

How Do You Process?

Beyond basic learning style categories, advanced coaching must also consider cognitive processing preferences that affect how people think about and approach problems. Sequential processors prefer step-by-step approaches and clear, linear progressions through skill development. They appreciate detailed explanations, logical organization, and systematic building from simple to complex concepts.

Sequential learners typically respond well to the structured approach of the **GREAT** Sales Coaching framework, appreciating the clear steps and logical progression from one skill to another. They often benefit from detailed checklists, systematic practice schedules, and coaching conversations that break complex skills into manageable components that can be mastered individually before being combined.

Global processors, conversely, need to understand the big picture before focusing on details and may prefer to jump around between different aspects of sales skills rather than following rigid sequences. They often become impatient with detailed step-by-step approaches and prefer to understand overall concepts and relationships before drilling down into specific techniques.

Global learners often benefit from coaching conversations that begin with discussions of overall sales philosophy and Customer relationship strategies before moving into specific tactical skills. They may also prefer variety in their practice sessions rather than repetitive focus on single skills, and they often appreciate seeing connections between different techniques and how they work together as integrated approaches.

Personality differences also significantly affect coaching effectiveness and require different approaches for optimal results. Introverted team members may prefer one-on-one coaching sessions and need more processing time before providing responses or feedback. They often benefit from advance notice about coaching topics so they can prepare mentally for discussions, and they may feel more comfortable with written feedback in addition to verbal coaching conversations.

Extroverted team members typically thrive in coaching environments that include discussion, social interaction, and immediate verbal processing of ideas. They may prefer group coaching sessions or peer learning opportunities and often benefit from coaching approaches that allow them to think out loud and process concepts verbally during sessions.

The challenge for coaches is creating environments that work well for both introverted and extroverted team members when working with mixed groups. This might involve providing options for both group and individual activities, allowing processing time for introverts while providing discussion opportunities for extroverts, and using varied coaching formats that engage different personality preferences.

Detail-oriented learners focus on precision, accuracy, and comprehensive understanding of techniques before attempting application. These learners often ask many questions during coaching sessions and may prefer written materials that they can reference during practice. They typically benefit from coaching approaches that provide complete information about techniques, including theoretical background and research support when available.

Big-picture learners focus on overall strategies and may become impatient with detailed tactical instruction. They often benefit from coaching conversations that connect specific techniques to broader business objectives and Customer relationship goals. These learners may prefer coaching approaches that allow for creativity and adaptation rather than rigid adherence to prescribed techniques.

Coaches working with detail-oriented learners should be prepared to provide comprehensive explanations, answer numerous questions, and supply reference materials that can be studied independently. Those working with big-picture learners should emphasize connections to broader goals, allow for creative adaptation of techniques, and avoid getting bogged down in excessive detail that might lose their interest.

Cultural Differences Matter

Cultural backgrounds significantly influence learning preferences and must be considered in advanced coaching approaches. Some cultures emphasize collaborative learning and may prefer coaching approaches that include peer interaction and group problem-solving. Others prioritize individual achievement and may respond better to one-on-one coaching focused on personal skill development.

High-context cultures may prefer indirect communication styles and may be uncomfortable with direct feedback or what they might perceive as confrontational role-play scenarios. Low-context cultures may prefer explicit, direct communication and may become impatient with approaches that seem too subtle or indirect.

Coaches working in culturally diverse environments need to develop cultural intelligence that allows them to adapt their approaches while maintaining effectiveness. This might involve varying communication styles, adjusting feedback approaches, modifying role-play scenarios to be culturally appropriate, or providing different types of recognition and reinforcement based on cultural preferences.

Age and generational differences can affect learning preferences and coaching effectiveness in ways that require thoughtful consideration. Younger team members may be more comfortable with technology-enhanced coaching tools and may prefer faster-paced learning environments. They might respond well to gamification elements, social learning platforms, and mobile-friendly resources.

Older team members might prefer more traditional coaching approaches and may need additional support when new techniques conflict with well-established habits and preferences. They might benefit from coaching that explicitly acknowledges their experience and expertise while introducing new concepts as enhancements rather than replacements for existing skills.

Multi-generational coaching requires sensitivity to these different preferences while avoiding stereotypes or assumptions about what different age groups prefer. The key is remaining flexible and responsive to individual preferences regardless of age, while being aware that generational patterns do exist and can inform coaching approaches.

Experience levels require different coaching approaches regardless of learning style preferences. New team members typically need more comprehensive skill building and may benefit from structured approaches that provide clear guidance and frequent feedback. They often appreciate detailed explanations, multiple examples, and patient support during the initial learning phases.

Experienced team members often prefer coaching that focuses on refinement and advanced techniques rather than basic skill development. They may become impatient with approaches that seem too elementary and may prefer coaching that acknowledges their expertise while introducing new concepts as advanced techniques rather than basic requirements.

The challenge for coaches is accurately assessing experience levels and adjusting approaches accordingly. Sometimes people with extensive experience in other fields may need basic coaching in retail sales techniques, while relatively new team members may have previous experience that allows them to move more quickly through basic concepts.

Motivation, Assessment, and Flexible Implementation

Motivation factors also influence learning effectiveness and should be considered when designing personalized coaching approaches. Some team members are motivated by competition and may respond well to coaching that includes performance comparisons and achievement goals. Others are motivated by mastery and prefer coaching focused on personal improvement and skill development. Still others are motivated by contribution and respond best to coaching that emphasizes how their improved skills benefit Customers and team success.

Understanding individual motivation patterns allows coaches to frame development activities in ways that resonate with each team member's driving forces. Competitive individuals might appreciate performance metrics and achievement recognition, while mastery-oriented people might prefer detailed skill development and personal progress tracking.

The assessment of individual learning preferences requires careful observation and thoughtful questioning rather than relying solely on learning style inventories or personality tests. While these tools can provide useful starting points, they shouldn't substitute for ongoing observation of how team members respond to different types of information, which coaching techniques generate the most engagement and learning, and what types of practice activities lead to the best skill retention and application.

Effective assessment involves observing engagement levels during different types of coaching activities, asking team members about their preferences and what works best for them, experimenting with different approaches and monitoring results, and remaining flexible and willing to adjust based on feedback and observations.

Flexible coaching approaches that can be adapted based on individual responses and preferences are more effective than rigid adherence to predetermined methods. Effective coaches maintain toolkits of different techniques and approaches that they can select based on individual needs and situational factors. This flexibility requires coaches to develop competence across multiple coaching modalities rather than specializing in single approaches.

The integration of different learning approaches often produces better results than focusing exclusively on preferred learning styles. Most complex skills benefit from multi-modal learning experiences that engage visual, auditory, and kinesthetic channels simultaneously. Advanced coaches learn to blend different approaches within individual sessions and across coaching programs to maximize learning effectiveness.

This integration might involve using visual aids to support verbal explanations, providing hands-on practice opportunities for concepts that were initially introduced through discussion, or combining individual and group learning activities to engage different personality preferences within single coaching programs.

Technology can enhance personalized coaching when used appropriately to match individual preferences and needs. Visual learners might benefit from video-based learning platforms and interactive infographics, while auditory learners might prefer podcast-style training materials or voice-recorded feedback. Kinesthetic learners might respond well to mobile apps that provide practice opportunities and immediate feedback.

However, as I keep saying over and over (sorry) technology should enhance rather than replace human connection in coaching relationships. The most effective approaches use technology to supplement personal interaction, provide additional learning resources, and create opportunities for practice and reinforcement that wouldn't otherwise be possible.

The measurement of personalized coaching effectiveness requires attention to both learning process indicators and performance outcomes. Process indicators might include engagement levels during coaching sessions, retention of information between sessions, willingness to attempt new techniques, and satisfaction with coaching approaches. Outcome indicators could include skill demonstration in practice sessions, application of techniques with Customers, and improvements in sales performance.

These measurements help coaches understand which approaches are most effective for different types of learners and enable continuous improvement of coaching methods based on results rather than assumptions about what should work.

Long-term development of advanced coaching skills requires coaches to continuously expand their repertoire of techniques and approaches while developing better abilities to assess individual learning needs and preferences. This development often involves formal training in different coaching methodologies, peer learning with other coaches, systematic reflection on coaching experiences and outcomes, and ongoing study of research on learning and development.

The ultimate goal of advanced coaching techniques is not just improved sales performance, but the development of team members who become self-directed learners capable of continuous improvement throughout their careers. When coaching approaches match individual learning preferences and needs, team members develop stronger learning skills, greater confidence in their ability to master new challenges, and increased ownership of their own professional development.

This transformation from external dependence to internal motivation represents the highest achievement of coaching excellence—creating people who continue growing and developing long after formal coaching relationships conclude.

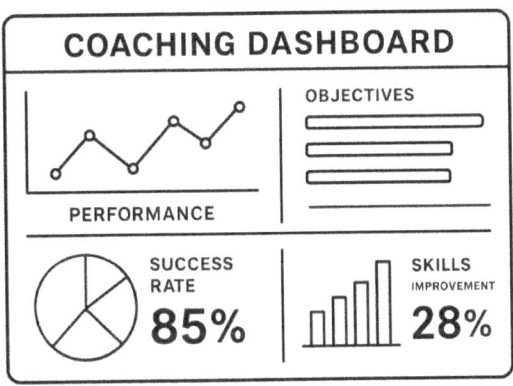

Chapter 12

Measuring Success - Metrics That Matter in Sales Coaching

If you've ever tried to lose weight, you know the frustration of stepping on a scale only to find that despite eating well and exercising regularly, the numbers haven't budged or worse, they've gone up. Yet your clothes fit better, you feel stronger, and people are commenting on how great you look. This common experience illustrates a crucial truth about measurement: the most obvious metrics aren't always the most meaningful, and the most important changes often can't be captured by a single number.

Understanding Measurement Complexity and Leading Indicators

The measurement of coaching effectiveness presents similar challenges and opportunities. While sales results provide obvious outcome measures, they don't tell the complete story of coaching impact, nor do they provide the granular feedback necessary to improve coaching methods and maximize return on investment. Sophisticated measurement systems must balance leading indicators that predict future success with lagging indicators that demonstrate business impact, while also capturing the qualitative changes in team capability and organizational culture that may be coaching's most valuable long-term contributions.

The complexity of coaching measurement reflects the complexity of human development itself. Unlike manufacturing processes where inputs and outputs can be precisely controlled and measured, coaching involves changing human behavior, which is influenced by countless variables including individual motivation, personal circumstances, organizational culture, market conditions, Customer demographics, and seasonal business patterns. This complexity doesn't make measurement impossible, but it does require more sophisticated approaches than simple before-and-after comparisons.

KPIs Tell Us What But Not Why

Traditional sales metrics such as revenue per salesperson, conversion rates, average transaction size, and units sold remain important measures of coaching effectiveness, but they represent only the tip of the measurement iceberg. These lagging indicators tell us whether coaching is working, but they don't provide insight into why it's working, which coaching elements are most effective, how coaching methods might be improved to achieve even better results, or whether observed improvements will be sustained over time.

The challenge with relying solely on traditional sales metrics becomes apparent when we consider the numerous factors that influence sales performance beyond individual skill levels. Market conditions, product availability, competitive pressures, pricing strategies, promotional activities, and seasonal patterns all affect sales results in ways that might mask or distort the impact of coaching efforts. A coach whose team shows modest sales improvements during a difficult market downturn may actually be achieving better results than a coach whose team shows larger improvements during favorable market conditions.

Leading indicators provide early signals of coaching impact and enable course corrections before problems become entrenched or opportunities are missed. These might include participation rates in coaching activities, demonstration of new skills during practice sessions, application of techniques in Customer interactions, team member confidence levels, peer-to-peer coaching frequency, or improvement suggestion submissions. Leading indicators help coaches and organizations understand whether their coaching investments are likely to generate desired business outcomes.

The identification of meaningful leading indicators requires understanding the causal relationships between coaching activities and business results. If coaching improves questioning techniques, and better questioning leads to more accurate product recommendations, which result in higher Customer satisfaction and increased sales, then demonstration of questioning skills during practice sessions becomes a valuable leading indicator of future sales performance.

The development of balanced measurement systems requires careful consideration of both quantitative metrics that can be tracked systematically and qualitative indicators that capture the human elements of coaching impact. Quantitative measures provide objective data that can be analyzed statistically, compared across different time periods or team segments, and used to demonstrate return on investment. Qualitative measures capture nuances of behavior change, cultural shifts, and individual development that numbers alone cannot convey.

The most effective measurement systems combine both types of data to create comprehensive pictures of coaching effectiveness. Quantitative data might show that average transaction values increased by 15% following coaching implementation, while qualitative feedback reveals that team members feel more confident in suggesting higher-value solutions and Customers appreciate the more consultative approach they're experiencing.

Individual performance metrics should track both skill development and business results to provide comprehensive pictures of coaching effectiveness. Skill development metrics might include competency assessments that measure specific technique mastery, behavioral observations that document application of coached skills, or self-assessment surveys that capture confidence and motivation changes. Business result metrics could include individual sales performance improvements, Customer satisfaction scores, productivity measures, or retention rates.

Easier Than it Sounds

The relationship between skill development and business results isn't always immediate or linear, which is why tracking both types of metrics is essential. Sometimes individuals demonstrate excellent skill development during practice sessions but struggle to transfer those skills to real Customer interactions. Other times, business results improve before skill assessments would suggest they should, indicating that confidence or motivation improvements are driving performance gains ahead of technical skill mastery.

The timing of measurement activities significantly affects their accuracy and usefulness. Measuring too early in the coaching process may capture temporary performance fluctuations rather than sustainable skill development. Measuring too late may miss opportunities to make mid-course corrections that could improve outcomes. Most effective measurement systems include multiple measurement points that track progress throughout the coaching process rather than relying on single before-and-after assessments.

Research in skill acquisition suggests that different aspects of learning develop at different rates and may require different measurement timelines. Basic technique adoption might be measurable within days or weeks of coaching, while advanced skill integration and natural application might require months to develop fully. Understanding these developmental timelines helps establish realistic measurement expectations and prevents premature conclusions about coaching effectiveness.

Team-level metrics provide insight into collective coaching impact and can reveal patterns that individual measures might miss. These could include overall team performance improvements, knowledge sharing behaviors, collaborative problem-solving effectiveness, or collective Customer satisfaction scores. Team metrics help distinguish coaching programs that improve individual performance from those that also enhance collective capability and organizational culture.

The analysis of team-level metrics can reveal interesting patterns about coaching effectiveness. Sometimes individual skill improvements don't translate into team performance gains because of poor collaboration or knowledge sharing. Other times, team performance improves more than individual improvements would predict, suggesting that coaching is creating synergistic effects where collective capability exceeds the sum of individual parts.

Customer feedback represents a crucial but often overlooked source of coaching effectiveness data. Customer satisfaction surveys, mystery shopping results, online reviews, Google reviews, and direct Customer feedback can provide valuable insights into how coaching improvements translate into enhanced Customer experiences. This external perspective often reveals coaching impacts that internal metrics might miss, such as improvements in Customer comfort levels, trust building, or satisfaction with service quality.

The collection of Customer feedback for coaching evaluation requires careful design to ensure that feedback relates to coachable behaviors rather than factors outside team member control. Questions should focus on interaction quality, service helpfulness, product knowledge demonstration, and other elements that coaching can directly influence, rather than general satisfaction measures that might be affected by pricing, product availability, or store policies.

The development of coaching-specific metrics requires understanding the unique aspects of skill development and behavior change that generic business metrics may not capture adequately. For example, tracking the speed of skill adoption, consistency of technique application, transfer of skills from practice to real-world situations, or retention of skills over time provides insight into coaching method effectiveness that sales results alone cannot provide.

Coaching-specific metrics might include the number of coaching conversations required to achieve skill mastery, the percentage of "coached" techniques that are successfully transferred to Customer interactions, the rate at which team members begin coaching each other, or the frequency with which team members seek additional coaching or development opportunities.

Baseline establishment is crucial for accurate measurement of coaching impact and requires comprehensive assessment of performance levels before coaching begins. Without clear understanding of starting points, it's impossible to determine whether observed improvements result from coaching activities or other factors such as seasonal variations, market changes, team composition shifts, or natural performance fluctuations.

Robust baseline measurement should include both individual and team performance data, skill assessment information, Customer feedback, and contextual factors that might influence results. This comprehensive baseline enables more accurate attribution of improvements to coaching efforts and helps identify which aspects of performance are most responsive to coaching interventions.

The attribution of performance improvements to coaching requires careful consideration of other factors that might influence results. Market conditions, product changes, competitive dynamics, team member turnover, promotional activities, and other business changes can all affect performance metrics in ways that might be mistakenly attributed to coaching. Sophisticated measurement systems attempt to isolate coaching impacts through control groups, statistical analysis, or other methods that account for confounding variables.

While perfect attribution is rarely possible in complex business environments, thoughtful analysis can provide reasonable estimates of coaching contributions to observed improvements. This analysis becomes particularly important when justifying continued investment in coaching programs or making decisions about program expansion or modification.

ROI, Technology, and Communication of Results

I know you will get this question at some point from your superiors as you implement the **GREAT** Sales Coaching framework. Return on investment calculations for coaching programs must consider both direct costs (coach time, materials, lost productivity during training, facility usage) and indirect costs (opportunity costs of alternative activities, administrative overhead, management time). Benefits should include not only immediate performance improvements but also longer-term impacts such as reduced turnover, improved employee engagement, enhanced Customer loyalty, and increased organizational capability.

The challenge with ROI calculations for coaching lies in quantifying benefits that may not have obvious dollar values, such as improved employee satisfaction, enhanced Customer experiences and relationships, or increased organizational adaptability. Some organizations develop methodologies for estimating the financial value of these intangible benefits, while others track them separately as important but non-financial outcomes.

The frequency of measurement activities should balance the need for timely feedback with the practical constraints of busy retail environments and the natural rhythms of skill development. Too frequent measurement can become burdensome and interfere with coaching activities themselves, while too infrequent measurement may miss important trends or opportunities for improvement.

Most effective measurement systems establish regular rhythms that provide adequate feedback without overwhelming participants. This might involve weekly check-ins during intensive coaching periods, monthly progress reviews during skill consolidation phases, and quarterly comprehensive assessments for ongoing development monitoring. The specific frequency should match the intensity and duration of coaching activities while respecting the time constraints of busy retail operations.

Technology can significantly enhance measurement capabilities when implemented thoughtfully and appropriately. Customer relationship management (CRM) systems can track individual and team performance metrics, learning management platforms can monitor skill development progress, performance dashboards can provide real-time feedback, and mobile applications can enable convenient data collection and reporting.

However, technology cannot replace human judgment and qualitative assessment in coaching measurement. While automated systems can efficiently track quantitative metrics, the interpretation of data and understanding of context still requires human insight and experience. The most effective measurement systems blend technological capabilities with human analysis to provide comprehensive and meaningful assessment of coaching effectiveness.

Use Benchmarks

Benchmark data from industry sources, peer organizations, or internal historical performance provides crucial context for interpreting coaching measurement results. Understanding how coaching improvements compare to typical industry performance, peer organization results, or historical organizational norms helps determine whether coaching programs are generating exceptional results or merely average improvements.

Benchmarking can also help identify best practices and improvement opportunities by comparing results across different coaching approaches, coach effectiveness, or organizational contexts. This comparative analysis can inform decisions about coaching method selection, coach development priorities, or program expansion strategies.

Communicate Your Efforts and Their Results

The communication of measurement results affects their impact on continued coaching effectiveness and organizational support. Different audiences require different types of information and presentation formats: detailed analytical reports for coaches and program managers, executive summaries for senior leadership, individual progress reports for participating team members, and team performance updates for peer groups.

Effective communication of measurement results should highlight both successes and areas for improvement while maintaining focus on continuous development rather than judgment or evaluation. The goal is using measurement data to improve coaching effectiveness and support continued learning rather than creating anxiety or competition that might undermine coaching relationships.

Continuous Improvement and Long-Term Validation

Continuous improvement of measurement systems requires regular evaluation of which metrics provide the most valuable insights, which measurement methods generate the most actionable feedback, and which reporting approaches are most useful for different stakeholders. This might involve retiring metrics that don't prove useful, adding new measures that capture important coaching impacts, or modifying measurement approaches based on experience and learning.

The evolution of measurement systems should be driven by their usefulness for improving coaching effectiveness rather than by measurement for its own sake. Metrics that don't contribute to better coaching decisions or improved development outcomes should be eliminated to focus attention and resources on measures that truly matter.

The integration of measurement activities with coaching processes helps ensure that measurement enhances rather than interferes with learning and development. When measurement becomes part of the natural coaching conversation rather than separate evaluation activities, it provides more authentic data while also reinforcing learning objectives and progress recognition.

This integration might involve incorporating performance metrics into regular coaching discussions, using measurement data to identify coaching priorities and success celebrations, or designing measurement activities that also serve as learning experiences for team members.

Long-term measurement systems should track career development, skill transfer to new situations, and leadership development among coached team members. These longer-term impacts often represent coaching's most significant value but may not be apparent for months or years after initial coaching activities conclude.

The tracking of long-term outcomes is more difficult since it requires maintaining contact with team members over extended periods and developing measurement approaches that can capture career progression, skill application in new contexts, and development of coaching capabilities in others. While challenging, this long-term perspective provides crucial insights into coaching's ultimate value and impact.

The validation of measurement systems requires periodic assessment of whether metrics actually predict desired outcomes and provide actionable insights for coaching improvement. This might involve correlating leading indicators with business results, comparing measurement data with qualitative observations, or conducting follow-up studies to determine long-term accuracy of early measurement results.

Without validation efforts, measurement systems may provide false confidence in their accuracy or mislead coaching decisions based on metrics that don't relate to desired outcomes. Regular validation helps ensure that measurement efforts contribute to better coaching rather than creating elaborate data collection systems that don't improve results.

The ultimate purpose of coaching measurement is not just to prove that coaching works, but to continuously improve coaching methods and maximize their impact on individual development and business results. When measurement systems achieve this purpose, they become powerful tools for organizational learning and continuous improvement that extend far beyond coaching programs themselves to influence how organizations approach all types of human development and performance improvement efforts.

The mastery of coaching measurement requires balancing analytical rigor with practical utility, ensuring that measurement systems provide meaningful insights without becoming burdensome or counterproductive. When this balance is achieved, measurement becomes a catalyst for coaching excellence rather than an administrative burden, driving continuous improvement in both coaching methods and business results.

Chapter 13

The Role of the GREAT Sales Coach - From Commanding to Developing

To finish this book, I wanted to spend some time talking about _you_ as the coach in the **GREAT** Sales Coaching process. The propose is to challenge you to evolve and grow not only your techniques, but also your philosophy and approach with your team. Most of you reading this book will be a sports fan like me, so I will use my observations from watching and playing sports to package the ideas.

The Coach

Imagine watching two basketball coaches during a timeout with their team trailing by ten points. The first coach storms onto the court, barks orders about plays that aren't working, criticizes mistakes from the last quarter, and sends the players back out with a stern warning about consequences if they don't turn things around. The second coach kneels down with the players, asks what they're seeing on the court, helps them recognize opportunities they're missing, builds confidence by acknowledging what they're doing well, and collaboratively adjusts the game plan based on their input.

Both coaches want the same outcome—to win the game. But their approaches represent fundamentally different philosophies about leadership, human development, and what it takes to unlock peak performance. The first operates from a traditional management mindset that relies on authority, control, and external motivation. The second embodies a coaching mindset that emphasizes development, empowerment, and internal motivation. The difference in their teams' responses—and long-term success—is typically dramatic.

This same distinction plays out every day in retail environments where leaders must choose between managing their teams or coaching them. While these roles might seem similar on the surface, they represent profoundly different approaches to human development that generate vastly different results in both performance and engagement.

The Manager: Playing the Numbers Game

Traditional managers operate much like old-school football coaches who believed in rigid playbooks and unquestioning execution. They focus primarily on results, compliance, and control. Their conversations with team members typically center around what went wrong, what needs to be fixed, and what will happen if performance doesn't improve. Like a football coach who only reviews game film to point out mistakes, managers often engage with their teams primarily when problems need to be addressed or policies need to be enforced.

As a DM, I once had a manager who told me "I'm not hear to tell you what you are doing right, I am here to tell you what you are doing wrong." While he was upfront with his philosophy and approach, it was demoralizing and demeaning. And it made me dread his coming to visit my stores.

The manager's toolkit consists largely of carrots and sticks—incentives and consequences designed to motivate behavior through external pressure. They might offer bonuses for hitting sales targets or threaten disciplinary action for missing goals. While these approaches can drive short-term results, they often create dependent relationships where team members perform only when being watched and rewarded, much like players who only hustle when the coach is looking.

Consider the basketball coach who draws up every play in detail, tells players exactly where to stand and when to move, and expects perfect execution without deviation. This approach might work against weaker opponents or in simple situations, but it breaks down under pressure or when unexpected challenges arise. Players become dependent on the coach's instructions or "system" and lose their ability to adapt and improvise when the game situation changes.

Traditional management approaches face similar limitations in today's retail environment. Customers are more sophisticated, competition is fiercer, and situations change rapidly throughout the day. Team members who've been managed rather than developed often struggle to adapt their approaches when scripts don't work or unexpected situations arise. They become like basketball players who can execute set plays perfectly in practice but fall apart when the opposing team runs an unexpected defense.

The fundamental flaw in pure management approaches is that they treat people as replaceable parts in a machine rather than unique individuals with different strengths, motivations, and developmental needs. This works fine when the job requirements are simple and unchanging, but becomes increasingly ineffective as roles become more complex and customer-facing.

The Coach: Developing Champions

Coaching represents a fundamentally different approach to leadership that mirrors what we see in sports where sustained excellence is the goal. Think about legendary basketball coach John Wooden, who focused more on developing his players as people than simply winning games. His teams won ten NCAA championships in twelve years not because he had the most talented players, but because he had a systematic approach to developing potential.

Wooden understood that sustainable success comes from developing people's capabilities, confidence, and character rather than just demanding better performance. His practices focused on teaching fundamentals, building mental toughness, and creating team cohesion. During games, his coaching was about helping players think through situations and make better decisions rather than micromanaging every move.

The coaching mindset starts with a fundamental belief that people have untapped potential that can be developed through the right support, guidance, and practice opportunities. Like a tennis coach working with a promising junior player, the sales coach sees current performance as just a starting point rather than a fixed limitation. They understand that with proper technique development, mental preparation, and consistent practice, dramatic improvements are possible.

This developmental perspective creates entirely different conversations between coaches and team members. Instead of focusing primarily on what's wrong, coaches spend most of their time exploring what's possible. They ask questions like "What would *you* like to get better at?" and "How can I support your development?" rather than "Why aren't you hitting your numbers?" The conversation shifts from problem identification to opportunity exploration.

The Sports Psychology Connection

Sports psychology research provides compelling insights into why coaching approaches are so much more effective than traditional management methods. Athletes who work with coaches focused on development and skill building consistently outperform those who work with coaches focused primarily on winning and external motivation.

The difference lies in what psychologists call "mastery orientation" versus "performance orientation." Mastery-oriented athletes focus on improving their skills and understanding of the game, while performance-oriented athletes focus primarily on winning, recognition, and avoiding failure. Research consistently shows that mastery-oriented athletes develop higher skill levels, demonstrate greater resilience under pressure, and maintain motivation longer than their performance-oriented counterparts.

In retail environments, team members developed through coaching approaches demonstrate similar advantages. They become more adaptable when facing unusual customer situations, more resilient when dealing with difficult interactions, and more motivated to continue learning and improving their skills. Like athletes who've been coached rather than just managed, they develop internal motivation that sustains performance even when external rewards aren't present.

Consider the difference between a gymnast who's been coached through years of skill development versus one who's been pushed to perform routines beyond their fundamental capabilities. The well-coached gymnast has solid basics, understands how different elements connect, and can adapt when something goes wrong mid-routine. The poorly coached gymnast might achieve short-term success but lacks the foundation to maintain performance under pressure or continue developing advanced skills.

From Referee to Skills Coach

One of the most profound shifts in moving from manager to coach involves changing from being a referee who enforces rules and judges performance to being a skills coach who develops capabilities and builds confidence. Referees focus on catching mistakes and applying consequences. Skills coaches focus on preventing mistakes by building better technique and understanding.

The referee mindset shows up in retail management when leaders spend most of their time monitoring compliance, correcting errors, and documenting performance issues. Like basketball referees, they're primarily reactive—responding to problems after they occur rather than proactively building capabilities that prevent problems.

The skills coach mindset approaches the same situations as development opportunities. When a team member struggles with customer objections, the referee-manager might document the problem and require improvement. The skills coach would analyze what's happening, identify specific techniques that could help, provide practice (role-play) opportunities, and offer ongoing support during the learning process.

This shift from reactive problem-solving to proactive skill building represents perhaps the most significant difference between managing and coaching. It requires leaders to think like athletic coaches who spend most of their time in practice sessions building capabilities rather than game officials who only show up to judge performance.

The Practice Field Advantage

Athletic coaches understand something that many business leaders miss: excellence is built in practice, not during performance. Which is why we have spent so much time in this book on the art of role-play. Basketball teams don't improve during games—they improve during practice sessions where players can experiment with new techniques, make mistakes safely, learn from failures, and gradually build muscle memory through repetition.

The coaching approach to sales development creates similar practice opportunities through role-playing, skill-building exercises, and safe learning environments where team members can develop techniques before applying them with customers. This practice-based approach contrasts sharply with traditional management methods that expect improvement to happen during actual customer interactions—the equivalent of expecting basketball players to develop new skills during championship games.

Consider how a swimming coach develops an athlete's technique. They don't wait until swim meets to provide feedback or expect technique improvements to happen during competition. Instead, they create structured practice environments where specific stroke elements can be isolated, practiced, and perfected before being integrated into competitive performance.

The **GREAT** sales coach applies similar principles by creating practice opportunities (pronounced role-play!) for specific skills like greeting techniques, questioning strategies, or objection handling. Team members can experiment with different approaches, receive immediate feedback, and build confidence in safe environments before applying new skills with actual Customers.

Building Mental Toughness

Athletic coaches understand that physical skills alone don't create champions—mental toughness and emotional resilience are equally important. They spend considerable time helping athletes develop confidence, manage pressure, bounce back from setbacks, and maintain focus during challenging situations.

The **GREAT** Sales Coaching approach to sales development includes similar attention to mindset and emotional skills. Sales coaches help team members build confidence in their abilities, develop resilience for handling difficult customer interactions, and maintain motivation during challenging periods. They understand that technical skills are only part of what makes someone successful in customer-facing roles.

This psychological development aspect represents another significant difference between managing and coaching. Managers typically focus on external behaviors and results, while coaches pay attention to the internal factors that drive sustained performance. Like athletic coaches who help players develop pre-game routines and mental preparation strategies, sales coaches help team members build the confidence and resilience needed for consistent customer service excellence.

The Team Captain Approach

Sports teams often identify certain players as team captains—individuals who demonstrate leadership qualities and help develop other team members. These captains serve as bridges between coaches and players, providing peer support and informal coaching that supplements formal development efforts.

The **GREAT** Sales Coaching approach to sales leadership includes developing similar peer coaching capabilities within retail teams. Instead of maintaining strict hierarchical relationships where development only flows from manager to employee, coaches create environments where experienced team members help develop newer colleagues and everyone contributes to collective learning. (Consider the triads tool discussed in Chapter 9.)

This peer development element creates what sports psychologists call "positive team chemistry"—an environment where team members genuinely want each other to succeed and actively contribute to collective performance. Compare this to traditional management environments where team members often compete against each other for recognition and advancement, creating internal dynamics that actually harm overall team performance.

The Championship Mindset

Perhaps the most profound difference between managing and coaching lies in their different definitions of success. Traditional managers often focus on short-term metrics and immediate results, much like coaches who are only concerned with winning individual games. While winning games is important, championship coaches think in terms of seasons, careers, and sustained excellence over time.

The **GREAT** Sales Coaching mindset in retail focuses on developing people who can adapt to changing situations, continue learning throughout their careers, and contribute to organizational success long-term. This requires patience with development processes, investment in people even when immediate returns aren't apparent, and faith that proper development will ultimately generate superior results.

Like athletic coaches who know that fundamental skill development takes time but creates lasting advantages, sales coaches invest in building capabilities that may not show immediate results but create sustainable competitive advantages through enhanced team capability and customer relationships.

The Legacy Question

Athletic coaches often measure their success not just by championships won, but by the impact they've had on their players' lives and careers. The greatest coaches are remembered for developing people who went on to achieve excellence in their own right, often becoming coaches themselves and passing on what they learned.

The **GREAT** Sales Coaching approach to retail leadership includes similar long-term perspective. **GREAT** sales coaches find fulfillment in developing team members who become confident professionals, effective leaders, and advocates for continuous learning and development. They understand that their greatest legacy lies not in the sales numbers they achieved, but in the capabilities they developed in others.

This legacy perspective creates entirely different approaches to daily leadership activities. Instead of focusing primarily on immediate results, coaches think about how current development efforts will benefit team members throughout their careers. They make decisions based on long-term human development rather than just short-term business metrics.

Making the Transition

The shift from managing to coaching requires fundamental changes in identity, daily practices, and measures of success. Like an athlete transitioning from player to coach, it demands learning new skills while letting go of old approaches that may have been personally successful but aren't effective for developing others.

This transition often feels uncomfortable initially because coaching requires patience with development processes that management approaches would try to shortcut. It demands faith in people's potential when current performance might suggest otherwise. It requires investment of time in activities that don't generate immediate results but build long-term capabilities.

However, leaders who successfully make this transition often find it profoundly rewarding. Like athletic coaches who discover that developing champions is more fulfilling than being one, retail leaders often find that helping others achieve excellence provides deeper satisfaction than achieving individual success.

The coaching approach doesn't abandon concern for results—championship coaches care deeply about winning. But it achieves superior results through different means, focusing on developing the capabilities that make excellent results inevitable rather than just demanding better performance from existing capabilities.

The Ultimate Victory

The true test of coaching versus management approaches becomes apparent over time. Teams that are managed might achieve short-term success through external motivation and control, but they often struggle when those external factors are removed. Teams that are coached develop internal capabilities and motivation that sustain performance regardless of external circumstances.

Like the difference between athletic teams that fall apart when their coach leaves versus those that maintain excellence through leadership transitions, retail teams that are truly coached become self-sustaining learning organizations that continue developing even when formal coaching relationships end.

This sustainable excellence represents the ultimate victory of the coaching approach—creating people and corporate cultures that are antifragile, growing stronger through challenges rather than just surviving them. The investment required to achieve this transformation is substantial, but the returns—in both human development and business results—make it one of the most valuable leadership capabilities any retail professional can develop.

The choice between managing and coaching isn't just a tactical decision about leadership style—it's a fundamental choice about what kind of impact you want to have on the people you serve and the legacy you want to leave in your profession. Like the difference between being a referee and being a championship coach, it determines whether you'll be remembered for enforcing standards or for developing champions.

Postscript

As we reach the conclusion of our journey through the landscape of **GREAT** Sales Coaching, it's worth reflecting on the transformation that occurs when organizations commit fully to developing their people rather than simply managing their performance. The principles, frameworks, and techniques outlined in this book represent more than just a collection of coaching methods—they embody a fundamental philosophy about human potential and the responsibility of leadership to unlock that potential.

Throughout these pages, we've explored the science behind effective coaching, the art of building trust and rapport, and the systematic approaches that turn good intentions into measurable results. We've examined the psychological barriers that can prevent learning and the cultural conditions that enable continuous growth. Most importantly, we've seen how coaching creates ripple effects that extend far beyond individual skill development to influence team dynamics, organizational culture, and ultimately, business performance.

The retail industry continues to evolve at an unprecedented pace, driven by changing consumer expectations, technological disruption, and competitive pressures that show no signs of abating. In this dynamic environment, the organizations that will thrive are those that can adapt quickly, innovate continuously, and maintain strong relationships with their Customers. These capabilities don't emerge from better systems or processes alone—they come from people who are engaged, skilled, and committed to excellence.

The **GREAT** Sales Coaching framework provides a roadmap for developing such people, but its success depends entirely on the commitment and skill of the leaders who implement it. Coaching is not a program to be rolled out or a checklist to be completed—it's an ongoing commitment to human development that requires patience, persistence, and genuine care for the people being served.

As you begin or continue your journey as a sales coach, remember that mastery comes through practice, reflection, and continuous refinement of your approach. The first time you implement the **GREAT** framework, it may feel mechanical or artificial. This is normal and expected. With time and experience, the framework becomes internalized, allowing you to focus less on the process and more on the unique needs and potential of each individual you have the privilege to coach.

The impact of great coaching extends far beyond the immediate business benefits, important as those are. When you help someone discover capabilities they didn't know they possessed, overcome barriers that seemed insurmountable, or achieve goals that once felt impossible, you contribute to their personal and professional growth in ways that can last a lifetime. These individual transformations aggregate into organizational transformation, creating cultures where excellence isn't just expected—it's inevitable.

The responsibility of coaching is both humbling and inspiring. You hold in your hands the opportunity to shape careers, influence lives, and contribute to the success of every Customer who interacts with your team. This responsibility demands your best effort, your continued learning, and your unwavering commitment to the growth and development of others.

As you move forward, remember that coaching is ultimately an act of service—service to your team members, to your organization, to your Customers, and to the broader community that benefits when businesses operate with excellence and integrity. The time and energy you invest in becoming a great coach will return to you multiplied through the success and satisfaction of those you serve.

The journey of coaching mastery never truly ends. There are always new techniques to learn, different approaches to try, and deeper insights to discover about human motivation and development. Embrace this continuous learning as part of what makes coaching both challenging and rewarding. Stay curious, remain humble, and never lose sight of the fundamental truth that your greatest achievements as a coach will always be measured by the success of others.

The retail industry needs great coaches now more than ever. Your commitment to developing people, building capabilities, and creating cultures of excellence contributes to an industry transformation that benefits everyone—employees, Customers, organizations, and communities. The work you do matters, and the people you serve deserve nothing less than your very best effort.

Welcome to the ranks of those who choose to make a difference through coaching. The journey ahead is challenging but immensely rewarding. Your team is waiting, your Customers are counting on you, and your organization needs the capabilities you can help create. The time is now, the opportunity is clear, and the tools are in your hands.

Go forth and coach with confidence, compassion, and commitment to excellence. The future belongs to those who invest in people, and through great coaching, you have the power to shape that future one team member at a time.

References

I wanted you to know the books and articles that inspired me in the writing of this book.

Bandura, A. *Social learning theory*. Englewood Cliffs, NJ: Prentice Hall.

Brehm, J. W. *A theory of psychological reactance*. New York: Academic Press.

Corporate Leadership Council. *Driving performance and retention through employee engagement*. Washington, DC: Corporate Executive Board.

Dweck, C. S. *Mindset: The new psychology of success*. New York: Random House.

Edmondson, A. C. Psychological safety and learning behavior in work teams. *Administrative Science Quarterly*, 44(2), 350-383.

Ericsson, K. A., Krampe, R. T., & Tesch-Römer, C. The role of deliberate practice in the acquisition of expert performance. *Psychological Review*, 100(3), 363-406.

Fournies, F *Why Employees Don't Do What They Are Supposed to Do and What To Do About It* McGraw Hill

Hudson, M. *GREAT selling: Building relationships and increasing sales through proven techniques*. Retail Training Solutions Press.

Hudson, M *Culturrific! The Roadmap to a Terrific Experience Culture*

Kotter, J. P. . *Leading change*. Boston: Harvard Business School Press.

Lombardi, V. *Coaching for teamwork*. In T. Dowling & V. Lombardi (Eds.), *Run to daylight!* (pp. 45-67). Englewood Cliffs, NJ: Prentice-Hall.

Senge, P. M. *The fifth discipline: The art and practice of the learning organization*. New York: Doubleday.

Skinner, B. F. *Science and human behavior*. New York: Macmillan.

Vygotsky, L. S. *Mind in society: The development of higher psychological processes*. Cambridge, MA: Harvard University Press.

Whitmore, J. *Coaching for performance: GROWing human potential and purpose* (4th ed.). London: Nicholas Brealey Publishing.

About the Author - Matthew Hudson

Dr. Matthew Hudson brings over three decades of sales excellence and organizational transformation expertise to his work as an executive leader, author, and master sales trainer. With a PhD in Organizational Behavior, he uniquely combines hands-on business experience with academic rigor to help organizations create sustainable, experience-driven cultures that deliver remarkable results.

Throughout his career, Matthew has guided startups through their critical evolution into stable corporations, accumulating over 10,000 hours of sales training and more than 1,000 coaching sessions. His proven methodology has helped architect successful sales processes for numerous U.S. corporations and associations, consistently driving revenue growth while fostering positive cultural transformation.

Matthew has had the privilege of working with industry leaders including Dell, New Balance, Absolute Software, and Disney, bringing his expertise in sales process design, corporate culture transformation, and scalable growth infrastructure to organizations of all sizes. As an author, he has written eight books covering sales methodology, signage optimization, and corporate culture transformation, plus two children's books that showcase his creative versatility.

Beyond his corporate work, Dr. Hudson demonstrates his commitment to community impact through his founding of six non-profit organizations. He currently serves as President of the Layla Rose Ranch Horse Rescue in Texas, embodying the same leadership principles and passion for positive transformation that drive his professional endeavors.

www.ingramcontent.com/pod-product-compliance
Lightning Source LLC
Chambersburg PA
CBHW051103160426
43193CB00010B/1301